Contents

THE INCLUSIVE LEADERSHIP BLUEPRINT

THROUGH HER EYES

The 4C Model: A Business Fable

DEEPIKA DABKE

ISBN
Paperback 979-8-89724-925-1
Hardcase 979-8-89744-960-6

Acknowledgments

As I sit to pen this section, my heart is filled with gratitude for numerous individuals who have contributed to my being. My mother, Aparna Bhide - a woman of extraordinary resilience and unwavering positivity - has been my biggest inspiration. She has shaped me in every possible way, and I know that my mother and father, Umesh Bhide, are watching over me from the parallel world, blessing me with their love.

My friend and life partner, Hemant Dabke - you have been the wind beneath my wings. Your ability to stand by me at all times and broaden my horizon of thinking is a gift that I will always cherish. To my daughter, Anushka - you have been my confidante and accountability partner throughout this literary journey. I feel eternally blessed to have you in my life.

I owe my gratitude to Sandhya Ramesh, General Manager - DEI, Godrej Consumer Products Limited, and Maithily Bhupatkar, - Diversity, Equity and Inclusion Practitioner, – you opened the world of Diversity, Equity, Inclusion, and Belonging (DEIB) for me. Collaborating with you gave me invaluable exposure to the ground realities of gender inclusion and opportunities for co-creating solutions to strengthen inclusion. I will forever cherish your friendship.

My passion for leadership was ignited and kept alive due to countless discussions and interventions that I undertook with my mentor- Mr. Jagdish Iyer, Director of Sytec Associates India Pvt Ltd. His encouragement and belief in my potential to contribute meaningfully to the field of Learning and Development became a guiding force for me throughout my career. I owe him my deepest gratitude.

Among the remarkable women leaders I have been privileged to learn from, Ms. Keyuri Singh, Management Consultant and ex-Vice President of Human Resources, Infogain India Pvt Ltd, has been my source of inspiration. Your generous investment of time and energy in my growth has profoundly impacted me. I remain indebted to you for the abundant love and knowledge you have shared with me selflessly.

The struggles and triumphs mentioned in this book are based on my interactions with numerous leaders and individuals that I met during various workshops, training sessions, and coaching engagements. I am deeply grateful to the participants and clients who allowed me a window into their realities, challenges, and aspirations.

To my lifelong friend Sulabha—you have been my pillar of strength, standing by me through thick and thin.

Many of my colleagues have been instrumental in keeping me on the journey of self-reflection and growth. Some of them took the time to review my manuscript and provide candid feedback, for which I am immensely thankful.

I express my gratitude to the Notion Press Media Private Limited team for all their support and guidance at every stage of the book publishing.

Our lives are often shaped by individuals we may never meet but whose work profoundly influences our thinking. I am grateful to the numerous authors, inspirational leaders, and personalities who have crystallized my understanding of leadership and guided me in building the 4 C model.

Finally, I am eternally grateful to the Almighty for showing me the path and bestowing the strength, courage, and purpose to bring this dream to life.

Introduction

Is The Inclusive Leadership Blueprint a work of imagination? Is it a fictitious story crafted to paint an idealized world? This book is a culmination of my experiences working with leaders and teams across industries who strive to build workplaces that are not just diverse but genuinely inclusive. The story of Indra reflects the challenges, aspirations, and transformations I've witnessed in organizations committed to building a safe and equitable environment for all.

Modern-day organizations are deliberate and distinct in building meaningful workplaces that attract diverse talent. From Google's groundbreaking initiatives like Project Aristotle and Project Oxygen to academic research conducted by Ivy League institutions and insights from global consultancy firms, one truth stands out: future-ready organizations must be inclusive. This being said, the everyday experience of inclusion lies mainly at the hands of their leaders. Thus, Inclusive Leadership becomes a critical element in the progress of contemporary organizations.

A friend of mine, a founder of a company that has experienced exponential growth in the last few years, confided that the modern-day leadership crisis stems from the leaders' deep-seated inability to adjust to the mindsets of modern teams. Leaders grapple with empathizing, and adapting to the new-age assumptions about leading and being led.

Meanwhile, small gestures and everyday interactions can make or break a team member's inclusion experience. A bright, high-potential woman once shared her disappointment when she realized she had limited access to her manager compared to her peers. It made her wonder if she would have the same opportunity for career progression. The challenges associated with inclusion are not limited to gender diversity alone. Many Gen Z employees' express frustration at being dismissed for their so-called "lack of experience" and are ignored or silenced.

These stories reflect the structural gaps and cultural blind spots that persist across industries with respect to engaging diverse teams. Many organizations pride themselves on articulating values of diversity and inclusion. They draft policies, roll out initiatives, and make public commitments. Yet, translating these intentions into tangible, everyday actions often fall short. Posters on walls, sporadic events, and PR materials do little to create a genuine sense of inclusion. The reality is that fostering inclusion requires more than surface-level effort—it demands consistent, deliberate actions, especially from leaders.

Despite these challenges, there is hope. Over the years, I have worked with leaders who are deeply invested in building psychological safety for their teams and creating an inclusive culture. These leaders have shown the courage to introspect, challenge their biases, and evolve to meet the needs of a diverse workforce. They have experimented with ideas, practices, and principles, often pushing themselves out of their comfort zones to create meaningful change. The 4C Model of Inclusive Leadership has emerged from these observations—a simple yet powerful framework to build an inclusive ecosystem. The Model provides a structure for leaders to reflect, realign, and act in ways that foster belongingness and trust within their teams.

As I first read Brené Brown's quote, "Maybe stories are just data with a soul," I realized that facts alone cannot inspire the deep, emotional connection needed to drive transformation. This book intentionally takes a story telling approach and weaves Indra's story into the framework to appeal not just to the head of the readers but also to the heart and the hands.

I once attended a program where the artists integrated Kathak, a classical Indian dance form, with contemporary choreography. At the end of the performance, the lead artist proposed that an impactful creation is a balance of structure and spontaneity. This metaphor deeply resonated with me. The 4C framework provides the structure to establish a culture of inclusion. Parallelly, the perceptions, biases and work realities bring spontaneity that poses challenges as well as opportunities to foster inclusion. The Inclusive leader blueprint tries to depict a dynamic interplay—a balance between intention and action, structure and spontaneity, and strategy and human connection.

While the protagonist of this book is a woman, the 4C Model of inclusive leadership transcends gender. It is a universal framework agnostic of the type of diversity within teams. Inclusive leadership is creating a workplace where everyone feels valued, respected, and empowered to thrive.

As you turn the pages of this book, I invite you to immerse yourself in the story and reflect on the framework. Experiment with the 4C Model. Challenge your existing leadership practices. Above all, embrace the journey of inclusive leadership—not as a final destination but as an ongoing commitment to learning, growth, and transformation.

Welcome to The Inclusive Leadership Blueprint. Let's begin.

PART 1

TURBULANCE

THE SHOCK

"Thank You Ajay…. Yes, of course… No, No… I understand, and I appreciate it." Indra could barely keep her voice steady.

The call came in at 11 A.M. on Tuesday, just as the grey clouds hung over the city and a drizzle blanketed the TechVista headquarters in Mumbai." …. Thanks again, Ajay."

As she placed her iPhone on the desk, Indra started rocking her chair absentmindedly, her eyes transfixed on the laptop screen, though her mind was far from the product roadmap she had been reviewing. "What just happened?" she mused. Just then, Indra received an email from HR with the subject line: "Congratulations, Indra! We are thrilled to announce that you have been named the new Head of Product Strategy & Innovation."

Her fingers hovered over the keyboard. Was this real? Indra glanced around her modest cabin, the wall behind showcasing her numerous certifications, the proud moments with her teams, the side walls adorned with pictures of her daughter, Rhea, and a quote she had pinned up years ago:

"Dreams don't work unless you do."

Indra didn't know what to feel. Her heart swelled with pride, but her mind filled with fear. Was she ready for this? Did she deserve this? William Shakespeare's quote flashed through her mind,

"All things are ready if our mind be so."

THE REACTIONS

While Indra was processing this development, her phone rang. "Shalini Finance calling". Indra knew what that meant. The word was out. TechVista had just announced to the world that she was in the driving seat.

Indra could sense a bead of sweat suddenly appearing on her forehead. How would everybody respond to this? Would they be happy? Would they appreciate the promotion as the outcome of her seven-year relentless efforts? Or would they whisper that she had snatched this opportunity from Anil, her earlier boss and one-time mentor?

"'Well, we will soon find out…" she said aloud, looking outside the window. The grey clouds seemed to have turned darker, the air a bit heavier.

That Wednesday morning, the news of Indra's promotion became a central theme of conversation. For some, it was a welcome change. "Finally, someone with a clear vision and conscience at the helm," Ravindran from the Sales team muttered to a colleague as they walked toward the coffee machine. But not everyone shared his optimism. Few were very skeptical of this move. "This is just setting Indra up for failure," one voice said, "Buying time until they identify someone from the industry." Another opined, "I don't think she has the brain or brawn for it anyway." The opinions oscillated from hope to despair.

"Hey, congrats, big girl." Priya, her close friend and colleague from pre-sales, entered Indra's cabin without knocking. As Indra watched her arrive, she neither tried to get up nor displayed any emotions. "We must celebrate," Priya continued.

"I don't know, ..." Indra started to protest. "Oh, come on..." Priya almost pulled her from her chair. "Get up, get up... let's start our celebration with a pastry." Priya was always up for a dessert.

"Who said pastry..." Indra turned to the door and saw Saumitra, her HR head, and their Diversity Equity Inclusion and Belongingness (DEIB) champ. Saumitra was a short, heavily built man with a heart of gold. Indra was incredibly close to him. He had been a great support and confidante during the past few months. "You knew this was coming, didn't you." Indra tried to fake anger but quickly broke into a smile.

"Well, you don't know how much effort I took to stop myself from spilling the beans." Saumitra chuckled and extended his hand to congratulate Indra.

"I am not sure, Saumitra. I don't think people would be happy with this." Indra voiced her inner fears to someone for the first time since the news was out. "Hey, don't say that? You deserve every bit of this promotion." Saumitra was gentle but emphatic.

"I hear you, Indra. If I were you, I would be worried. They are setting you up. Anyways, it's not about you. It's about optics." Indra was shocked. "Optics?"

"Of course," Priya said, her tone blunt but not unkind. "Elevating a woman to the leadership role is great for their diversity statistics. And Suresh? He's desperate to create a positive image. He'll try anything right now."

Saumitra stiffened. "That's unfair, Priya. Indra got this promotion because of her hard work and talent. She's exactly the kind of leader that this function needs."

Priya shrugged, "Hundred percent Saumitra. I completely agree." She glanced at Indra, "But I just think they're hedging their bets."

Indra sat there staring at the quote on her wall: 'Dreams don't work unless you do,' the words that always fuelled her seemed less appealing today.

She had no appetite for the celebration. She leaned back and sighed, her gaze drifting to the window. "Am I ready for this?" she thought.

THE FIRM

Few months ago, TechVista was not just another IT company; it was 'THE IT company.' Industry stalwarts proudly associated TechVista's name with innovation and agility. With the help of cutting-edge solutions and a strategic approach, TechVista made daring leaps into cloud-based enterprise solutions.

Suresh Menon, the CEO, had a clear purpose: expanding TechVista's operations within and outside the country. Thanks to the exceptional team of tech specialists, TechVista made a mark in the BFSI and Healthcare space.

As the firm grew from 200 to a whopping 2000 employees, the company's culture underwent a massive change. Competition became stiff, and work pressures increased. Clients became more impatient, demanding, and less forgiving.

The past few months have been exceptionally stressful for everyone at the company. TechVista witnessed several client escalations, technical snags, and irregularities with key accounts. The data breach at AMD Finance seemed like the last straw on the camel's back. TechVista's once-unshakable confidence was now wavering. The company's future hinged on its ability to regain trust, deliver results, and, most importantly, lead with clarity.

DREAMS, DESIRE, AND DETERMINATION

For Indra, TechVista was more than a workplace. The seven years she spent here were a journey of transformation. Born into a modest Bengali family, Indra's parents always encouraged her to build her capabilities in the academic and extracurricular world.

"You are my lucky star," Indra's dad, Atanu Dutta, would proudly tell her. He was the wind beneath her wings. Her academic excellence landed her in St Joseph College of Engineering, one of the best Shivapur, a small town near Nagpur, could offer. She was an excellent student and one of the few students who got a campus placement in a firm in Nagpur.

"How can she move to Nagpur alone? Where will she live? "Rohini was not ready to let go of Indra. But Indra's dad was adamant. "Oh, stop it, Rohini. People are leaving their country for better prospects, and you want to chain your daughter and prevent her from going 200 kilometres away? We have given her a strong foundation and deep values. And now it's time for the bird to leave the nest." There was no appeal after that assertion.

The bird did fly, and there was no looking back. Four years later, Indra was sitting in TechVista's office in Mumbai. She joined the company as a Product Analyst. Indra was an ambitious young woman, always dreaming of making it big and making her father proud. Moving from a non-metro to a bustling metro city was a challenge, but she embraced it head-on. With no godfather or mentor to guide her, she knew that hard work and perseverance would be her only ticket to success.

During her early days in Mumbai, she met Akhil Mohan through a common friend. A CA by profession, Akhil worked with a PE fund. Akhil was calm, composed, and quiet, the opposite of Indra's bubbly, restless, and anxious soul. Within a year of knowing each other, they decided to tie the knot and co-create a life they dreamt of.

The following two years brought a share of joy and deep pain. Indra lost her dad, her most incredible support in life, to stage four pancreatic cancer. Her mother was devastated. In less than two weeks after her dad's demise, Indra realized that she was pregnant. "Life is such a mixed bag," her heart ached.

"Ma, you should come and stay with us," Akhil insisted, and Indra's mom, Rohini, graciously accepted the invitation. The next few months were a struggle to manage home, health, and work.

Once Rhea was born, life became sweet and complicated, all at the same time. Akhil was an incredible partner and a doting father, and Ma was a fantastic support. Yet, juggling the family and work role was challenging. While TechVista had shown patience with her, she had to pay a price for the "absence" from work in the form of losing a due promotion. However, she did not allow this decision to dampen her spirits. She knew she would have to rebuild her reputation from scratch.

She worked hard, grew as the Senior Product Manager, and became a critical member of the product team led by Anil. "One day, I will succeed Anil and be the Head of this division." She had vowed.

Today, she was fulfilling that dream. Yet the feeling was more of dread than happiness.

ON YOUR MARKS, GET SET

Suresh Calling, the screen of her iPhone, lit up with the name of her CEO and Suresh's image built in front of her eyes in a flash.

In looks, Suresh Menon was no less than a movie star. He was 6 feet 4 inches tall, fair, and a handsome man with a booming voice. Whenever Suresh entered the room, heads turned. He commanded a fair bit of attention and respect in the industry, and everyone at TechVista would keep their respectful distance from him. Indra had not interacted with him much in all these years until the fateful incident.

"Good morning, Suresh." Indra tried to sound cheerful on the call.

"Congratulations, Indra. I hope you are ready for this." Suresh's voice seemed cold.

"Yes, of course, Suresh. Thank you so much for believing in me and giving me this opportunity." Indra meant every word she said.

"Hmm. Coud you please come to my office immediately? Ajay and I would like to speak with you." Suresh was curt.

Ajay Arora was the Chief Product Officer (CPO) at TechVista and an old-timer. Rumour mills suggested that he had once been the right-hand man of the earlier CEO, Raj Shekhar. Over time, however, his prominence had faded, and many felt he was merely biding his time, waiting for the sun to set on his long-drawn career. After Anil's sudden exit, Indra and her lateral colleague Rajiv reported directly to Ajay.

Indra hurriedly shut her laptop, got up, straightened her somewhat crumpled blue jacket, picked up her diary, and headed to the elevator to go to the 27th floor. In the elevator, she caught her reflection in the mirror and sighed, wishing she had taken a moment to straighten her hair or add a touch of makeup. "Whatever, Indra, you are not a candidate; you are already in the driver's seat. Be yourself." Her inner dialogue asks her to focus and stay calm.

Suresh's office was a simple yet elegant corner room overlooking the green race course. The Mumbai skyline stood tall against the patch of green. Today, the grounds were drenched, and the outside mood looked sombre. The energy in the office was relatively muted.

"Hello, Indra. Congratulations!" Both men rose and took their turns to shake hands with Indra. Once the pleasantries were over, the mood immediately turned morose.

"Indra, you have been with the firm for almost seven years. You know what we have gone through lately. Business is bleeding, and we are facing backlash from all sides."

"Yes, Suresh, we are all concerned. We have a great team here, and I am sure we can turn the tide with your guidance and Ajay's support," Indra added with conviction.

"And we must do it sooner than later, Indra…" Suresh did not seem interested in what Indra had to say. "I won't lie to you." Suddenly, Suresh seemed very stern and distant. "Your appointment met with a fair number of objections and concerns. The board was quite divided between you and Rajiv. Some still believe Rajiv was the safer choice. Others—" his lips curled slightly—" Let's say, I made a bold decision by picking you, Indra." Indra shifted in her chair uncomfortably. Ajay, sitting one chair away, seemed to be unbothered.

"They'll be watching every move you make, Indra. And so will I." Indra's stomach tightened. She took a deep breath and said it with as much conviction as possible. "I understand the scrutiny, Suresh. I'll do my best to prove you right."

Suresh's expression didn't soften. "Proving me right is the bare minimum. I would like you to fix the ProMax mess and fix it fast. This is our last shot at regaining credibility in the healthcare market. You need to get down to business ASAP and revert with a blueprint of how we will get out of this mess. I don't want to lose a single client from now on."

Indra had been in the role for less than 30 minutes and could already feel the heat. "Suresh, I will do my best. You know me. Ajay also knows my level of commitment." was all she could manage. She maintained a calm exterior and an air of assurance, "I will soon work on this with the team and prepare a blueprint by Monday morning."

"No, Indra, I need it by Friday morning." Suresh demanded.

She glanced at Ajay, hoping he would say something in her support. But he made no such attempt. "But it's Wednesday today, Suresh… I have not even met my team after the elevation," her voice trailed off. Suresh leaped up and perched on the table, leaning over her. "Indra, you are an old player. You can create a blueprint in an hour if you decide to. I think you will need to buck up on this one. So, just get going. Some of the board members will also be present during the Friday meeting, and they will expect answers. And don't forget Indra, the board is watching you."

Indra became silent. Her shoulders dropped, and she looked away. She shut her diary and got up. There was no point banging her head against this wall. I will be ready." she mumbled and left. Priya's words echoed in her head. This wasn't just an opportunity but a gamble that could define or destroy her career.

THE CRISIS

The crisis was one of the worst that TechVista had witnessed. They had launched ProMax, an end-to-end solution to serve their premium customers in the Banking and Health Care segment, four months earlier with much fanfare.

The product was supposed to be TechVista's ticket to meteoric success. But the launch was just the beginning of a saga. Four months after the launch, the very foundation of trust on which TechVista stood came crashing down. It started with whispers of a breach—then exploded into a full-blown cyber-attack. The hackers had infiltrated TechVista's cloud infrastructure, exposing sensitive financial records and patient health information. The fallout was catastrophic. This incident created terrible news in the market. The mega healthcare client threatened to file a lawsuit against TechVista, accusing them of negligence in data protection measures. The news of the breach spread like wildfire, and within 48 hours, TechVista's stock price plummeted by 15%.

Indra and a few others knew they were sitting on a ticking bomb. They had pushed for additional investment in cybersecurity measures. But Anil Dalal, Indra's boss, opted to deprioritize these concerns. The last few months made him look like a mediocre leader who failed in vision, trust, and integrity. He was only bothered about profit maximization and dismissed any concerns about data security and its vulnerability in the face of cybercrimes. Indra had consistently shared her concerns and highlighted the risks involved. But Anil always preferred to follow Rajiv's advice and almost reprimanded Indra for delaying the process. She tried to raise red flags but finally gave up. "Stop complicating things," were Anil's words in a meeting when Indra had tried to push harder." "These are hypothetical risks. We can address them later." Anil had thrown a lousy fit in one of the meetings. But 'later', it never came.

Indra documented the concerns and left it at that. After the breach, Suresh and the board formed an internal committee to analyse the root cause. There were lots of irregularities and oversights. Indra's documentation led the team to unearth a lot of concerns and challenges. The committee established that Anil had ignored multiple flags raised by the cybersecurity team for enhanced protocols. They appreciated Indra's efforts to raise concerns and highlighted a need for more significant risk mitigation measures. Many believed that Indra was the reason for the final nail in the coffin for Anil. The fact that the board's criticism of Anil was mainly on the backdrop of Indra's report weighed on her mind and somehow made her feel guilty.

Today, when Indra confided in Saumitra and shared her feelings, Saumitra challenged her, "Why are you behaving as if you are confessing to murder? Anil faltered Indra. He let his judgment fail him. You can't bury yourself in guilt and pressure over something that wasn't your doing." Saumitra was almost scolding Indra. And Gautam Buddha's quote flashed through Indra's mind,

"Your worst enemy cannot harm you as much as your own unguarded thoughts."

THE HOT SEAT

People were unsurprised at Anil's resignation, but the leadership crisis was evident. The senior leadership had to urgently fill the Head of Product Strategy & Innovation position. The choice came down to two candidates;

Indra, known for her analytical thinking and foresight, had been instrumental in stabilizing operations during the breach. Over the years, she had earned a reputation for being committed, loyal, and outspoken. However, some viewed this last virtue as a tendency to be too aggressive and challenge authority.

Rajiv on the other hand was Anil's former protégé. Anil had always positioned Rajiv as someone with prowess in managing high-stakes product development activities and launches. However, Rajiv's inability to anticipate the security issues related to ProMax and the subsequent breach raised serious doubt about his capabilities.

The board and senior leadership were divided on the choice of candidate. The pro-Rajiv faction believed Rajiv's familiarity with the product line made him a safer choice. "We also need strong leadership representation in the market currently. Would

Indra be able to create the necessary space for us? After all, the best of the world's economies have rejected women as leaders, fearing they may be unable to garner support on important issues." Nobody could deny this strong logic in the backdrop of global political examples.

The pro-Indra faction contended that her ability to foresee risks and adapt under pressure made her the stronger candidate. "We should give a chance to deserving people." was the moralistic argument.

In the end, it was a hung parliament. The jury could not reach a consensus, and the ball was in the CEO's court. That evening, as Suresh sat in his swanky apartment on Marine Drive overlooking the sea, the last few months' events flashed through his mind. "Anil was surely a bad breed," he thought. He had not come to terms with the fact that his judgment had failed him so badly. After all, Suresh had strongly recommended Anil and was instrumental in convincing him to join TechVista.

There were many red flags, but Suresh failed to see them. Anil's charm and smooth talk had tricked him into taking his eyes off the goalpost. Now, it was time to make things right. Many rode on this decision, and he could not afford to go wrong.

Suresh could think of many reasons to elevate Indra. He had watched Indra accomplish remarkable success over the past few years. Her loyalty to the company was unquestionable. Despite her disappointment in not getting what she deserved or desired after her maternity break, she had not considered quitting. She put her head down, gave her best, and worked relentlessly to help TechVista succeed.

On the other hand, Rajiv was more confident and charismatic, something the company desperately needed in its leader. But he was Anil's blue-eyed baby, "which means he was either the cause of some of the issues that emerged or a contributor to the mess." Suresh mulled over the matter.

Elevating Indra also had its political advantage. By making this choice, TechVista looked progressive and an equal-opportunity employer. The sentiment that meritocracy was compromised during Anil's reigns would also die down. Indra's selection was a strategic gamble.

Suresh seemed to feel safe playing this wild card.

THE TEAM

The day was hectic for Indra. She spent a significant part of the day drawing up priority lists, checking the status of ongoing projects, and bumping into random people greeting her with appreciation, smiles, and best wishes. After numerous calls, emails, and meetings, Indra finally decided to focus on the team meeting she was looking forward to and, in many ways, even dreading the most.

Indra knew that the team would have mixed reactions to this development. She had booked Orion, a spacious conference room with a large oval table and ample space to move around. The long French window and the Mumbai skyline added to the room's beauty.

As Indra waited for the team, Aditi walked in. With her 5 foot 7 inches lean self, Aditi looked radiant in an elegant red dress with a delicate flowery scarf. She leaped forward to hug Indra. "Many congratulations, Indra. I am so happy for you. This is surely the most deserving promotion I have seen coming through in a long time." Aditi's tone exuded genuine happiness and excitement.

Aditi Sharma, the product innovation lead, was one of the younger team members and always radiated enthusiasm and hope. However, confidence was not her best friend and Indra had informally mentored her from time to time. Aditi had often felt stifled under previous leadership but saw Indra's promotion as a chance for change. "Finally, someone who might back my ideas," Aditi thought, her optimism barely contained. "We could create something amazing together!"

Just then, Naveen, the Data Analytics Manager, and his work buddy Vivek, Senior Engineer, entered the room.

"Indra…." Vivek's big, booming voice filled the room.

"Congratulations, so how does it feel…"

"Thanks, Vivek. I am still coming to terms with it, honestly."

Everyone noticed Indra's authenticity and vulnerability. "Hmm, I am sure you will take to this role like a fish to the water," Naveen said with a poker face.

Naveen Deshmukh. It was always tricky to figure out this man. Naveen had spent some time in the US and returned to India to care for his parents. He enjoyed his time at TechVista as it gave him time to focus on his start-up idea during the weekends. Besides, his wife headed the Food and Beverage section at a highly accomplished chain of restaurants and had a very demanding schedule. The flexibility offered by TechVista ensured that Naveen could be with their 5-year-old twin boys and balance the life part of the equation. He had seen leaders come and go and would hardly ever get blinded by their aura. "She'll need to prove herself with numbers, not just words," Naveen thought, drumming the table softly with his fingers.

Vivek Joshi, on the other hand, was a more easy-going dude. Vivek would always stand out from the crowd due to his dressing sense. His casual polo shirt, relaxed posture, piercings, and innumerable tattoos gave him a very cool vibe. As a Senior Engineer, he brought tremendous value to what he did. But Vivek was not too bothered about what happened at work. He was due to get married in August to his childhood sweetheart, Shuchi, and did not care about office politics. He looked at Indra and thought, "I'll support her if she shows she knows what she's doing, but no leader ever survives without listening to the Engineers." His face flashed a quick smirky gaze before his regular, sweet dude expression returned to his face.

"No way, bro; how did you manage that?" Sneha was heard asking Dave. As they entered, it was clear that Dave had managed to get the tickets for the weekend performance of some Gen-Z sensational band. Indra smiled at them and waited for them to settle. "Hey, sorry guys, are we late?" Sneha looked sheepishly at others. "Of course not, mademoiselle. We, the lesser mortals, can always wait for you till eternity." Vivek chided and threw a naughty glance at Naveen. "So, you agree that you are lesser than me," Sneha said with a brazen face.

"What are those tickets for?" Naveen quickly changed the subject. "Aare nothing , some Josh or something… band coming to town." Dave chuckled.

"Don't say some, bro…." Sneha looked hurt. "They are THE Brand.." Her eyes twinkled, "..and Dave managed to get one ticket for me." She was beaming. Dave just smiled and slipped into a corner chair, far from where Indra was standing.

Dave Mendonsa was the Quality Assurance Lead. He was 31 years old and wore a straight-jacketed, formal attire that mirrored his meticulous personality. Dave was a perfectionist who believed in high standards and zero compromises. Thanks to his role, most people considered him a pain and would try to push back on his insistence on process adherence and compliance. Dave had also been very vocal about the irregularities during the ProMax launch, but no one other than Indra had taken him seriously. In that sense, Dave wanted to extend his full support to Indra. "As long as the products meet my quality benchmarks," Dev thought; Dev was already typing away on his laptop, his testing scripts filling the screen. "Let's see if she can deliver."

Sneha Patel was a 23-year-old cheerful, outspoken, and somewhat impatient UX designer. She aced her work and was very confident about what she brought to the table. Sneha had completed her master's course at NYU and had joined the world of work more as a distraction from her otherwise "dull life" in the South Mumbai neighbourhood. She was excellent at her job and had razor-sharp eyes on everything that happened with and around her. That evening, she sat with her apple pencil and iPad, doodling design concepts as the meeting began. Her purple-streaked hair and bohemian jewellery stood out. "This team is stuck in its old ways for too long," Sneha thought, her pen scratching across the screen. "I hope Indra shakes things up. We need that."

As they were taking seats, Indra was feeling very nervous and tense. Rajiv, her biggest competitor until yesterday and supposedly her biggest challenge from today, was missing. "What are you going to do now? What if he draws swords from day one itself? Are you going to let it pass?" Her head was reeling; a storm of thoughts stirred in a teacup.

"Hey, did anyone see Rajiv?" Indra tried to sound as casual as possible. She felt the room went silent for a few seconds until someone volunteered to ping him. Just then, Orian's door opened, and Rajiv stood there.

Rajiv Kapoor, Senior Product Manager, was a 6 feet 4 inches tall, fair-skinned, handsome young man who moved around with an air of importance. His physique stood testimony to his inclination towards fitness. Indra had heard that Rajiv never compromised on his gym schedule and worked out at least 2 hours every day. As a marathon runner and state-level national champion, one would expect Rajiv to have a sporting spirit. But that was hardly the case. He was a poor loser with almost zero sporting spirit. Be it a fun game of TT in the recreation room, a presentation at the client site, or a bet over a cricket match, Rajiv would always make everything about himself.

Rajiv was Anil's prodigal son. The duo had built a fortress around them, which was difficult for others to penetrate. During the ProMax debacle, this closeness had prevented Anil from fully embracing the situation. He based his decisions on the myopic view that Rajiv brought to the table. ProMax had been a career-limiting move for Anil and, eventually, for Rajiv. The only difference was that Anil was out while Rajiv was still in. "I won't give up so easily," he had vowed while reading the HR mail this morning. He knew Indra was walking on thin ice, and he had every intention of shaking the surface so that she would slip.

The energy of the room changed the minute Rajiv walked in. He strode off with an air of indignation. With crossed arms, Rajiv sat listlessly, avoiding Indra's gaze. Instead, he chose to scroll through the content on his phone with deliberate disinterest. "Let's see how long she lasts," Rajiv thought, his smirk barely hidden. "I'll give her a week before she cracks under pressure."

Indra had two days to work with this team and build a blueprint. The question was, will she make it?

DRAMA BEGINS

"**G**ood afternoon, everyone," Indra began, sounding cheerful although she could feel the pressure internally. "I know this has been a turbulent time for all of us. TechVista has never been under the weather, and now that we are where we are, the company needs our care and attention like never before."

She paused, unsure whether to say what she was about to say, "I also know some of you may have reservations about me stepping into this role." Indra paused a bit longer and looked around. Vivek looked away. Dave glanced at Vivek, and Rajiv kept staring at her coldly. Aditi nodded in the negative, dismissing the thought. Suddenly, she let her gaze rest on Rajiv and continued. "But here's the thing: I'm not here to dwell on the past. I know each one of you has given your best to this company and would never like to see it crumbling. We have an incredible team here and some remarkable products to offer. I do not want to throw in the towel just yet. Let's make TechVista a leader in the market again." There was a pensive silence in the room.

Sneha broke the silence, "Indra, I am with you on the vision part. However, ProMax's roadmap has many gaps. How are we supposed to deliver it on time?"

Indra nodded, acknowledging the concern. "You're right. We have inherited a flawed roadmap. Our priority is to rebuild the path." Just as Indra felt she had caught the team's attention, Rajiv jumped in, "That sounds good in theory, Indra. But we do not know how long you will need to settle in the role before you can come close to rebuilding." he chuckled. His comment reeked of sarcasm.

Indra chose to ignore the remark and continued. "I know transitions can be challenging, but I am confident we will survive this one. Let's explore all ideas and balance innovation with practicality. I need each of you to identify the biggest risks in your areas by tomorrow."

"Woh, that's such a short time, Indra. What do you want us to do? Camp in the office and work for 24 hours?" Rajiv smirked.

Indra was beginning to get tired of Rajiv's high-handed attitude. She crossed her arms, stood straight, and replied, "Rajiv, the ProMax issue is something we have analysed and processed numerous times in the past two weeks. We must simply decide what the project needs from our expert standpoint and draw a blueprint."

Rajiv interjected indignantly, "Indra, just for the record, we have a strategy in place. I can fill you in on the critical pieces and make sure you're up to speed." He was not going to let the ball drop.

Indra shuddered at his patronizing tone. She responded, "Thank you, Rajiv. I will look at the strategy, and we will decide as a team if any course correction is needed. It can't be two people running the show and the others paying the price of their shortcomings."

The room went silent. Indra regretted her words the moment she said them. Everyone knew what she was hinting at. And Indra had to be better than this. She could not let the shadows of the past eclipse the chances of the future.

CELEBRATION

After the team meeting, Indra dove into countless transactions. Around 7.30, a call from Akhil got her to acknowledge the ticking clock and her aching back.

"Hey, have you left… I will be home in 10 minutes." Akhil loved to reach home early and spend some time with Rhea. That also helped Ma to go for the evening walk and catch up with her friends from the complex.

"Arr, no, I am just about to leave. I should be home in an hour." Indra did not even want to consult Google Maps, knowing she could not make it home before 9 P.M. "Why don't you guys finish dinner and wait for me?" Indra tried to get as much positive punch as she could in her voice.

"Sure, see you at home then." was the end of the conversation. It was not unusual for her to skip dinner with family. Her mom disapproved of it, but Akhil understood. "It's a man's world, Indru," Akhil would keep telling her. "I know you have to work two hundred percent to get half the respect of your male colleagues." Sitting in her cab, she fondly thought of Akhil and felt blessed to have him by her side.

After a two-hour Uber ride, she entered her modest but well-maintained apartment and found the family enjoying Rhea's favourite movie, Lion King. When Rhea noticed her enter, she leaped up and ran towards Indra. Indra could feel her tiredness melting away.

Rohini, Indra's mom. She looked up from her magazine and smiled at her, "Hello beta, ki korcho?" (What do you do). Then, glancing at her, she added, "If you're not going to eat on time twice a day with family, what's the use of all this wealth?" Indra did not have the mental strength to counter her mom. Akhil sensed the tension and interjected to lighten the mood.

"Who is in for ice cream after mom has her dinner?"

"Today's treat is on me," said Indra. "Aare Wah, that's great," Akhil replied without much inquiry. "Don't you want to know why it is on me?" Indra smiled naughtily. "Oh, is there something you are not telling us?" Akhil looked up while picking up Rhea's storybooks.

"Hmm, maybe." Enjoying the suspense, Indra continued. "What is the news, beta?" Rohini suddenly got curious.

"You are talking to the Head of Product Strategy & Innovation." Indra said with pride, a feeling she was allowing herself for the first time in the day.

"Wow, Indru! That's huge—congratulations!" Akhil jumped up and hugged her.

"What does that mean?" Rhea asked, never one to like feeling confused. "Mom got promoted, sweetie." Akhil explained with a note of pride in his voice. "Oh, ma, congratulations!" Rhea hugged her and gave her a long kiss. "Thanks, love." Indra responded. She felt her eyes fill with tears and a lump form in her throat. Suddenly, the day's heaviness seemed to have vanished.

After a brief celebration, the household became quiet. Indra put Rhea to bed and sat beside Akhil. "I am very proud of you, Indru." Akhil said with warm eyes that could melt a glacier. "Why didn't you call me earlier?" He seemed a bit hurt. "I wanted to, Akhil… but this promotion comes with a lot of baggage." Indra narrated the day's events to him and poured her heart out—her fears and disappointments.

"I don't know if I can fill these shoes, Akhil. I do not feel ready."

"You feel that way because you think from your 'female brain' Indru." "Ohh, come on, Akhil." Indra protested.

"No, I am serious." Akhil continued. "I mean, look at Rajiv. He has goofed up and yet has the cheek to believe he deserves this role more than you. This is your game, Indru. Do not let someone take it away from you. Even worse, do not make a self-goal. Don't you quote Sheryl Sandberg: "Don't leave before you leave" from her book Lean In?"

Indra took a deep breath, "But I have no one to lean on, Akhil. You need someone to lean on from time to time before you lean in."

"I know you, Indra. You're a fighter, and I know you will be a winner." Akhil's voice carried deep conviction. Indra wished she had shared Akhil's optimism.

Part

2

CROSSWIND

BURNING THE MIDNIGHT OIL

Despite Akhil's soothing words and the cheerful celebration, Indra could not shake off the feeling of dread building within. Sleep, usually her best friend, had also turned her back on Indra. "The Friday presentation isn't just about the project blueprint; it's a test of my ability to lead, win over skeptical stakeholders, and prove my worth."

Suddenly, she got out of bed and returned to her study. She quickly immersed herself in the 30-odd-page report and started putting down her thoughts on the existing strategy, timelines, and resource allocation plan to identify gaps or missteps. "I have to win over my internal client first and then the external." She sighed, her thoughts returning to the afternoon team meeting. Somewhere in the wee hours of the morning, she drifted off to sleep, only to wake up to her shirking 5:30 A.M. alarm.

"Time to embrace the day, Indru." She pushed herself into the kitchen, ready to prepare Rhea's tiffin, pack her to school, and play the Head of Product Strategy & Innovation.

THE DRAMA CONTINUES

The next day's meeting in Orian looked no different. Interestingly, the same people were seated in almost the same spots. Once everyone was in, Indra stared with an enthusiastic pitch, "I have been looking at ProMax data and thinking about our next steps. I mailed the meeting agenda and some notes yesterday night. I hope you have been able to see it."

"2 A.M., Indra. Seriously? What were you even thinking? Are you going to work a double shift now?" Naveen cribbed, rolling his eyes. Indra made a note, "Do not email the team after eight unless necessary," she vowed. "Remember, eight is too late."

After a quick briefing, Indra turned to Rajiv, who sat at the far end listlessly. "Rajiv, could you update us on our progress on the cybersecurity ramp-up and provide your insights on our immediate next steps?" She tried to keep her voice calm.

"Well, I have already shared my thoughts and given my input during the audit." Rajiv shrugged. The energy in the room suddenly changed. People stopped and looked at Indra to see her reaction to this cold start. "Why don't you walk us through that plan and add the feasibility angle?" It was taking every ounce not to show her irritation and anger.

Reluctantly, Rajiv got up from his seat, attached his machine to the projector, and started speaking. "Frankly, the data analytics team could have done better." Indra could almost see Naveen straighten in his chair, his facial muscles contriving.

"Wait a minute, what do you mean?" Naveen snapped.

"I mean, with all the data and access to intelligence that you and your team had, you didn't do enough to raise the red flag." Rajiv was enjoying the effect he was having on Naveen.

"Excuse me, but if you had bothered to review the email trail from the past three weeks before Anil's departure, you wouldn't be saying this right now. It's funny how you have led us into this mess and want to shirk the responsibility now." Naveen's eyes blazed. Rajiv was livid. "Watch your words, man. I am not going to sit around and take all the blame."

Indra observed the growing tension in the room. The fragility of their team's relationship was on full display. Until now, no one had openly challenged one another, but the cracks were opening with the slightest pressure.

Indra had to intervene, "Folks, calm down. Let's focus on our next steps rather than bicker and play blame here." Twenty-five minutes into the meeting, they had reached nowhere.

"We also need to look at some product innovation steps." Anjali was unsure if she should speak or wait for the wind to die. "Ohh, come on Anjali. Please do not try to add value where not necessary." Vivek cut Anjali off. Anjali lost momentum and kept quiet.

Sneha suddenly got up. "Hello, folks. Can we stop fluttering from one topic to another? I don't want to be stuck in this stupid room all day and hem and haw about this stupid presentation."

"This presentation is not 'some stupid' presentation, Sneha." Indra's voice was flat, the ring of anger evident for anyone who cared to notice. Sneha backed off a bit. "The future of this product and our account is hanging on this one." Indra added, more to herself than to others.

Without wasting much time, she regained her focus and took charge of the room. "Here is what we are going to do now." Indra's changed demeanour took everyone aback. In the next hour, all the groundwork needed for the initial draft was ready. People were more focused and resourceful this time, and by 7:30 P.M., the blueprint looked quite promising.

Work was accomplished, but the team seemed disengaged. Indra knew she would have one more sleepless night. After all, tomorrow was her 'Agni Pareeksha,' Baptism by fire, as one may call it.

THE MEETING

Friday morning, the city rose to one of the wettest days of the season. The rains had been incessant since the night before. Not wanting to be late, Indra skipped breakfast and dashed to work. Just as she entered the lobby, she noticed Ajay emerging from the parking lot. "Good morning, Ajay." she greeted him and held the elevator door for him to enter. Ajay hesitated for a moment and then joined her. "Big day today." He smiled at her. "Yes, the team has worked hard to create a blueprint. I mailed it to you yesterday. Did you get a chance to look at it?"

Ajay seemed confused. "Uh... no... uh… I didn't quite check my mail yesterday evening." he said nonchalantly. "Of course, it was also quite late when I sent it." Indra did a good job hiding her disappointment. "Could we review it once to ensure I have nailed all the points? I want your guidance and opinion." Indra said earnestly.

By then, the door had opened to get her off her floor. "Ohh, you will be fine. Let's meet at 3 P.M.," was all Ajay said. Indra's spirit almost wilted. But she did not have time for such touchy-feely matters. There was too much on the plate, and Indra could not spare much time on the meeting or the blueprint for most of the morning. By 2.45 P.M., Indra had gone through her presentation for the Nth time and felt slightly confident.

Indra was the first to enter Aquarius, a beautiful oval-shaped room partly overlooking the green race course. She had fond memories of Aquarius, but today, its charm failed to bring a smile to her face.

As she settled in a chair two places away from the centre seat, she caught a glimpse of Ajay, Suresh, and Bhaskar walking towards the room. They exchanged pleasantries, and soon, two team members from the Legal department joined them. Two more board members, Mario and Shekhar, joined the group. Just as Indra thought they would start, to Indra's dismay and shock, she saw Rajiv entering the meeting room. Her heart sank.

"I am glad you could make it at such short notice, Rajiv," Suresh said pleasantly to him. "No problem, boss." Rajiv was beaming. He looked in Indra's direction, gave her a long, triumphant look, and settled.

"All right, gentlemen," Suresh stopped and looked at her, "and the lady, of course," he added. "We are here to review the ProMax issue and look at the way forward. A lot of water has flown over that bridge, and I do not want to take any chances. Many of our clients who are already using the platform have raised concerns. Some have even threatened to terminate the contracts. Many may be contemplating but have not raised the flag yet. Therefore, we must look at the steps to consider for the coming months." Suresh paused. "Indra, now that you have taken over the role, we can turn the ship around under your leadership."

Indra could feel her body tense. She got up and moved towards the projector. "I hope so, Suresh." It was a weak start, everybody noticed. While she adjusted her machine to project her presentation, Suresh added, "Rajiv, you have been an integral part of this journey. I thought it would be a good idea for you to attend the meeting. We can surely use an extra brain here to make headway."

"I will surely do what I can," Rajiv said confidently and smiled. Indra thought of what Akhil had mentioned earlier about the difference between men and women. "Well, gentleman..." and she began. Indra delivered a well-rehearsed pitch. Although frazzled by Rajiv's presence, she continued to dive into the charted-out data points. "Can I ask a question?" Indra paused and looked at Bhaskar, who had meticulously taken notes for the past 15 minutes. "I appreciate the level of detailing you have done, but I am unclear on the part that covers meeting such stringent deadlines."

"I would like to explain," Rajiv interjected. For the next five minutes, he explained the same points that Indra spoke of. To Indra's horror, people sat in rapt attention, listening to him. "...And that is how we will make the plan feasible." Rajiv concluded and glanced at Indra. Indra could see the nods at the table.

"What I don't understand." Indra noticed Mario, who had been quiet for most of the meeting, got up and paced around the room. "If you have such a superior understanding of the matter, Rajiv, what stopped you from averting this matter?" Mario looked at Rajiv pointedly. The room went silent. Indra sat silently, taking in what had just happened.

"During Anil's time, you had presented a way forward, which did not reflect any of the thoughts you shared today." Mario's piercing eyes once again rested on Rajiv. Now, Rajiv had become visibly uncomfortable. "I am happy that you reiterated the points that Indra made in her presentation, and I am sure you will extend all your cooperation while she gets us back in the game." Mario had directed these words more as a threat. "Of course, Mario. I am here because I care." Rajiv showcased his most sincere look. "That's good because we don't expect anything less now," Mario concluded. "You may continue, Indra."

Indra looked at Mario with gratitude, gathered herself quickly, and continued. The twenty-five minutes that followed witnessed the most invigorating discussion that TechVista had for a while. All the preparation served Indra well, and she laid down a clear road map in front of her audience. Heads nodded, smiles returned, and there were a few fleeting moments when Suresh seemed thrilled with what Indra was proposing.

Indra could sense that she had passed the acid test. The war was not over, but she had salvaged the day. As she sat, a smile returned on her face.

"You don't have to see the whole staircase; just take the first step." the words of Martin Luther King Jr came alive for her.

THE SAGA CONTINUES

If someone thought this would be an 'I came, I saw and conquered' moment for Indra, that was far from true. The next three weeks involved a herculean task of keeping the momentum going. Each day was a new test for Indra.

To start with, there was a technology failure at RDBC bank, causing a sense of panic at TechVista. Suresh was livid. "Indra, have you cared to assess the situation? Could you tell us what went wrong?" Indra kept a calm exterior and began firmly. "This project has seen a significant integration challenge, and we should have supported each other better. For example, if we look at the tech support...."

With that, Hari, the Head of Technology, jumped in. "Oh, integration challenge? Tell me more about it." Without wasting a breath, he turned to Ajay. "You and your team are the ones steering the product strategy. You have not foreseen this risk. Now, you cannot turn it on, my team." Indra could not help but admire how Hari dove to protect his team. She knew she could not expect any support from Ajay. "Hari, I understand your frustration. It is not about foreseeing risks. It is about misalignment between teams and an unrealistic timeline, which I raised multiple times. The failure was systemic, including lacking resources and support from other departments. So, we must pick our share of responsibility to be correct. "She looked at Ajay and then Suresh, pleading with them to stay focused on solution orientation. Therefore, I propose we put our heads together and devise a way forward. I have already set up a cross-functional task force to prioritize critical fixes. But the truth is, we need all of you to get on board to make this work."

At this, Hari exploded the second time. "Onboard? Are you serious? My team is facing the wrath here. How can you be so casual? We are not planning for some kitty party, Indra." The room went silent for a moment. Some mild chuckles and laughter were heard on one side of the table, but Indra was too shocked and angry at this remark.

"And what makes you think we are treating this like a kitty party, Hari?" Indra was furious. "How many times have you interacted with the client? Or gathered data? Have you fully understood where we stand legally on this issue?" She looked pointedly at Hari. He became uncomfortable with this direct attack.

"I have spent at least four evenings talking to various stakeholders, which, by the way, is not my job. So, I will not take lessons from anyone about taking ownership. Gentlemen, my team is doing everything they can, and we need support from the tech team now." By this time, Suresh decided to take matters in hand. "Indra, do you have a plan for how we can proceed?" His tone was softer and civil. Indra calmed down and said, "Yes, Suresh, I have some thoughts."

One hour later, each knew what they needed to do. But the meeting had taken a pound of flesh from Indra.

The next day was no different. Indra was having a mid-week review with the team. As usual, Rajiv and Naveen were giving her a tough time. Aditi and Sneha were disappointed in the chaos caused during the meeting. And Indra was slithering, wanting to strangle a few people at the table. Indra moved on with the review, but the fragmented energy remained. As the meeting ended, she saw they had finished with incomplete inputs, a muddled direction, and a growing frustration.

By 6.45, Indra was dead. Exhausted, she decided to close the day and go home. "Oh, home already?" Akhil was pleasantly surprised to see Indra at that hour. He was helping Rhea with her science project. "Now, you don't need to be sarcastic, Akhil." Indra snapped. "Hey, what do you mean? Who is being sarcastic?" Akhil snapped back. "Ohh," Indra clenched her jaws. "I get it. I am not doing enough to help with household chores or Rhea's work. But that doesn't mean you make it a point to humiliate me."

"Indru, breath, what on earth has gotten into you?" Akhil's ordinarily calm demeanour had changed. Rhea looked at her parents and was unsure of what to do. Rohini had come out of the kitchen and watched as her daughter and son-in-law seemed to be getting ready for a fight. And Indra just looked at them, "Forget it." and strode out of the room.

Indra was devastated. "These days, nothing seems right. Every interaction leaves me drained and bitter and angry." She lamented. As she sat at the table alone, scrolling through the Instagram reels to distract herself, she came across a quote by Mark Twain,

> ***"Anger is an acid that can do more harm to the vessel in which it is stored than to anything on which it is poured."***

She couldn't agree more. She was noticing it day in and day out.

THE INVITATION

"Hey, did I bother you?" Indra immediately recognized Saumitra's voice on the other end. "Hello!" Indra answered with a playful smile. "To what do I owe the honour of receiving a call from you?"

"I called you to check on how you will travel to the venue tomorrow," Saumitra said pleasantly. "What venue?" Indra was startled. "Hey, you are supposed to be speaking at the round table tomorrow, organized by the Women in the Tech World group, remember?" Saumitra seemed worried now.

"Ohh shit, I completely forgot about it." Indra could not believe she had overlooked the block in the calendar. "The last few days have been crazy, Saumitra. There is just so much on my plate… that I …"

"I understand, Indra," Saumitra said sympathetically. "But you don't have to worry. It is just a panel discussion. You will be fine." He continued.

"Saumitra," Indra pleaded, "Could you please do me a favour? Could you please call the organizers and excuse me from this affair? I don't want to do this." Indra's tone was desperate.

"I understand how you feel, Indra, I really do," Saumitra tried a softer approach. "This round table has great visibility in the industry. The PR around this is huge. Organizations are clamouring to be a part of this. We can't throw away our chance of being seen on this forum." Saumitra's voice was soft yet decisive.

"Why don't you send someone else, Saumitra?" Indra pleaded. "Whom do I send? There are hardly any women at that level, Indra. Plus, you are our best face now that you are elevated."

"Oh, please stop this tokenism, Saumitra. You want me to sit on this forum trying to show that TechVista is such an inclusive place when the ground realities are that women are being talked over and thrust into leadership roles more as a fall person." Indra blurted out. Suddenly, she realized that Saumitra had become silent on the other side. "I am so sorry, Saumitra. I have no right to talk to you this way," she said hurriedly.

"Hey, don't worry about that. I know how you feel, and I will not blame you. But Indra, Suresh has invested time and energy in getting us the spot at this event. I am not doing the name-dropping thing. But as a friend, I suggest you honour this commitment." Saumitra had nothing more to say.

This last reasoning was too compelling to dispute."Fine…. I will go." was all she could manage.

GETTING READY

Once it was established that there was no wriggling out of the event, Indra decided to pivot and rearrange her next day quickly. "Women in the Tech World" was an NGO working towards encouraging girls to take up STEM subjects and later commit themselves to the Tech world. For the past 6 years, they had been relentlessly carrying out training and mentoring activities for women, conducting events and activities centred around gender inclusion.

"So, would they print this interview in the newspapers?" Rohin, Indra's mom, wanted to know. "I don't know, ma," Indra responded drily. It will be shown on some news channels."

"Wow, so you are going to be a TV star," Akhil teased. Indra just rolled her eyes as she continued to braid Rhea's hair. "So, Rhea, you will be a star's daughter." Akhil continued the banter. "Akhil, stop having fun at my expense." Indra snapped at Akhil. "Oh, hello, now what did I do?" Akhil looked puzzled. "Why are you getting irritated? Where is the old Indra who would have two bits of her wits to display?" Indra just kept mum as Akhil got ready to leave with Rhea. Once the duo left, she returned to her chores.

"What will you wear?" Rohini enquired. "I don't know, Ma. I have not thought about it."

"Why don't you wear that tussar silk I got you during the last Durga pooja?" Ma got up enthusiastically. "I can find it and keep it ready for you."

"Nobody cares what I wear, Ma, and didn't I say this is no big deal?" Ma stepped back. Indra's voice had raised, and so had her temper. "I was just trying to help. You hardly seem to be paying attention to how you look these days. Look at all these young girls and how they carry themselves. I thought it would be …" Rohini mumbled, clearing the plates from the dining table.

"I don't have time for such trivial things, Ma. And I don't care how I look. And those other pretty girls do not have a boss breathing down their neck and a wasted team to manage," Indra continued to rant as she filled her lunch box.

"Fine, do what you like. And please try to spend some time with Rhea. She really misses you." The last sentence set Indra off. "Ohh, please don't get started, Ma. Why do you do this? Why do you always make me feel I am not good enough? No matter what I do, I always fall short of everyone's expectations." Indra was fuming, her lips curled up, brows raised, and eyes filled with tears.

Rohini was shocked and hurt. "I am just trying to help here. You are the one thinking such things and hurting yourself and us. Anyway, all the best for your event." Rohini looked at Indra painfully, picked up her house keys, and left.

Indra was shocked that she had thrown a fit for no reason. None of what she had said was Rohini's doing or, for that matter, Akhil's or Rhea's fault. She was acting out. She had to do better than this. She could not help but remember Mark Twain and his quote.

THE ROUND TABLE

Indra was one of the three speakers at the event. Dilkhush, a dear friend and a leading TV Anchor of a Business and Finance channel, was the moderator for the panel discussion.

"Don't worry, we will just have fun," she assured Indra when Indra shared her trepidation and lack of experience of speaking at such forum. The other panellists were ace speakers. Anushree was a CHRO of a leading automobile company and a celebrity, thanks to her recent book, 'Let your voice be heard.' The second panellist was a lady named Ojaswi Nayyar. She was a founder and Director of an NGO called Through Her Eyes Foundation (THEF), primarily dedicated to transformational work for women.

Normally, Indra would do homework on her co-panellists, etc., but this was not the right time for her. She was supposed to meet the group at 10 A.M. for a quick tea and chat, and then get on the dais at 11 A.M. Thanks to the Mumbai traffic, Indra could only reach the venue around 10:25 A.M.

The energy of the venue was quite appealing. As she entered the visitor's lounge, Dilkhush waved and urged her to join them.

Dressed in an elegant white jacket and striped blue trousers, Dilkhush looked radiant. Indra quickly shook hands with Dilkhush and Tanushree and turned to Ojaswi to exchange pleasantries.

Ojaswi's image was not at all what Indra had imagined. Five feet 4-inch, petite, whitish complexion lady, Ojaswi almost seemed to be her mom's age. She wore a beautiful white and red Kolkata cotton saree, an elegantly handcrafted gold and red beaded necklace, and a matching earrings. Something about the lady made you feel instantly comforted and peaceful. "Hello dear," her voice had a ring of magical calm. The four quickly dove into the questions and session outline and were ready to go on stage.

"OK, ladies, it's time to get started. OG, I want as many one-liners from you as possible, OK? They'll become a staple for my audience." Dilkhush showed a fake demandingness on her face.

"Yes, ma'am, you are the boss lady," Ojaswi replied cheerfully.

The next hour was one of Indra's most fulfilling hours in days. There was so much sharing and learning, and the audience had such brilliant questions! With all modesty, Indra thought she did her part very well. But the highlight was Ojaswi's stories, her profound understanding of women's psyche, struggles, and their triumphs. Indra was genuinely impressed by Ojaswi and the value she was creating for aspiring women through her NGO. And, of course, the one-liners were the highlight.

AWAKENING

OJASWI - THE OG

"You know OG originated as slang for gangsters in the 1960s, don't you? And yet, you all keep calling me that." Ojaswi was enjoying the banter. "And you are a gangster for all practical reasons, OG, just a cute one and a Gang-Stir; that's how you are making waves in gender inclusion. And you, indeed, are the OG for the voices less heard." Dilkhush was making no attempt to hide her admiration for Ojaswi.

"You were incredible, Ojaswi." Indra was mightily impressed by OG. "That was nothing." OG casually waved her hand. "In fact, you were so authentic. I would love to know more about your journey. Why don't we have a cup of coffee? I know a great cafe just around the corner," Ojaswi offered. "Of course, only if your schedule permits. I have the luxury of time, but not you young busy bees." Ojaswi quickly added.

"Ohh, I would love to…" Indra said enthusiastically. The moment the words came out of her mouth, she regretted. "What? I don't believe I just said that. And what about the R K group issue?" Her inner voice exploded. Indra was kicking herself, but something in her wanted to continue chatting with Ojaswi just a bit more.

OG and Indra quickly said their goodbyes to the organizers and left. In five minutes, they were seated at 'It's All About Coffee' a small, cozy, well-lit cafe. Ojaswi seemed a regular here. "Sharon, two of your Chef's special salad and some ginger lemon tea for us. Indra was pleased with the smoothness with which Ojaswi had befriended her and invited herself into Indra's world.

"So, what's about being called OG?" Indra teased. "Ohh, that is the ruckus that my young friends like you and Dilkhush started. They feel my name is too old-fashioned and even a bit boring." "Oh, no. Your name is lovely; it means the bright, radiant, enlightened one, right?" Indra inquired.

"Yes, at least that's what my parents expected of me when they called me that," Ojaswi said with twinkling eyes. "But today, I forget to respond if people call me Ojaswi." She chuckled.

"So, what made you start THEF?" Indra was curious. "Hmm, restlessness, I guess, and a strange sense of responsibility." OG's eyes softened as she looked at her and said with sincerity. "I was fortunate to get the best education and opportunities, Indra. My first job was with a personal healthcare MNC. They were very progressive with respect to gender inclusion. So, I quickly made it to the power corridors and became a national head in 11 years." OG seemed to be walking the nostalgic lanes.

"But along the way, I realized that not all were so privileged. Despite the conducive culture in my organization, women could not make the cut after one point." OG had a troubled look on her face. "The more I noticed, the more my heart ached." She paused.

"So, you just gave up your job and started the Through Her Eyes Foundation?" Indra asked admiringly.

"No, like most of us, I waited a few more years, expecting others to become change agents." She smiled. "Then, around 2013, I met a 26-year-old Irish woman working in the remote area near Bastar, educating women and making them employable. She sensitized the village Sarpanch (the village headman), coached and counselled girls, roped in their mothers, and worked hard to create a bright future for them. I asked myself, "Why can't I do this for my people?" and that was it. I gave up my job and started looking for the right set of people and the right cause to invest my time. Twelve years later, with 90-odd people joining my movement, I'm glad we have touched the lives of almost fifty thousand women from different walks of life." OG's words reflected a sense of responsibility rather than arrogance or pride.

 "I will never be able to make an impact as you do." Indra said more with shame than admiration. "Of course, you will. Young women like you amplify our cause and provide mentoring to our young girls. There are many ways of adding value, Indra, really…" OG was earnest but not pushy.

"Well, you're talking to someone who's struggling and trying to figure out her own life right now," Indra said, staring at her coffee. "Oh," Ojaswi exclaimed. "Life can be tough," she said softly. OG's authenticity made Indra melt; even before she could realize it, tears started flowing down her cheek.

OG reached across the table and took Indra's hand. A deep silence filled the air. Before Indra knew it, she was sobbing. In a minute or so, the sobs stopped." What's wrong with me?" Indra pulled away, embarrassed. "I'm sorry. I…" She spoke quickly; her words almost incoherent.

"No need to feel sorry, dear." Ojaswi's calm voice was once again working its magic. "I can see that you are not used to being this vulnerable, especially in front of a stranger." "I should go. I have already ruined your afternoon." Indra could die out of embarrassment. "Hey," OG's eyes softened, "It's OK to acknowledge what is going on inside. How else will you manage it?" Imagine a wound—green and raw on the inside—while flaunting smooth, flawless skin on the outside." Indra could not flaw that logic. She sat still.

"Indra, the inner world is a far more complex and challenging territory to conquer. The outer world is still manageable." Indra absorbed each word, realizing the power of this simple yet profound truth.

THE LISTENING CIRCLE

That day, Indra woke up from a deep slumber.

"Oh my god, how did I oversleep? What time is it, and how did the alarm not go off?" She leaped out of bed and raced towards the kitchen. Ma was seated at the table, reading the newspaper and sipping her usual ginger tea.

"What's the matter, Indru." her mom looked up.

"Ma, why did you not wake me up? It is already 7.30 A.M. Rhea has already missed her bus. Now I must take a detour and drop her to school. I am going to get stuck in that damn traffic." Indra whirled around the kitchen as she spoke.

"But don't you have a holiday today?" Rohini inquired. And then it dawned on Indra—it was the weekend. A Saturday morning. The week had passed in a blur. Indra felt a warmth rising within her—a whole weekend with Rhea and Akhil.

While Indra relaxed on the balcony with a hot cup of ginger tea, her thoughts returned to her chat with OG. "At THEF, we believe in sharing and being there for each other. In fact, we have an online Listening Circle this Saturday. I will send you a link.

I would love you to come, even for some time, and see what happens there." OG seemed very excited about the meeting.

Just then, she received a text. "I hope you are attending the Listening Circle." The Zoom link was shared with a personalized note.

"I think I should join the meeting, even if for some time," she thought. When she joined the Zoom link at 10:57 A.M., around 50 women had already joined. In the first 5 minutes, OG welcomed those who were new.

"The Listening Circle is a ritual followed by us to reiterate, reinforce, and celebrate our 4 C Philosophy of Inclusive Leadership practice." OG tried to provide quick context for those who were new. "We start by recognizing those of us who have tried to apply the 4 Cs in our daily interactions and have tried to create a larger impact." Five people were recognized for supporting or uplifting some women at the workplace or from the community. Each briefly explained the activity that had earned them the honour. Indra was amazed by the display of grace and gratitude in each sharing and the variety of the projects taken up for the advancement of women.

Next, they had a WIN segment:

Moments that went Well

Moments that conveyed a need for Improvement and

Moments that were invested in Nurturing someone.

Indra was quite surprised to see the range of sharing done by others. One young lady, Farha, volunteered to go first. "I have always avoided taking on tasks that feel overwhelming or risky.

It was not just fear of failure—it was fear of letting others down. But thanks to the second C, I have started pushing myself out of my comfort zone. Two weeks ago, when my manager asked for volunteers for a tough project, I did not overthink it. I just... put my hand up."

Next to share was Manek. "I have started something fascinating with my group to honour the third C. As a senior leader, I have always believed in creating inclusive spaces, but intentions do not necessarily guarantee actions. A few months ago, I started a practice with my team called "She Says, He Says." Every fortnight, we discuss how different genders might interpret behaviours, words, or gestures differently. This is a great exercise for building empathy for my team and me."

The entire cohort was listening in rapt attention.

Indra was floored, "Such wonderful sharing. I had thought of continuing for a few minutes but never realized how time flew." While Indra was processing all she witnessed, she heard someone summarizing the call and announcing the end of the meeting.

What is the 4 C that these folks are constantly harping about?" Indra wondered.

"WE MEET AGAIN"

"Thank you so much, Ojaswi, for inviting me this morning. It was amazing to hear everyone's stories and the wisdom being shared. I am curious about the 4 C philosophy. Is it a leadership tool? Is there any material I can read to learn more?" Indra sent a text to OG soon after the call.

OG replied almost instantly. "I'm so glad you could join, Indra! What makes you ask for the material?"

Indra hesitated for a moment before responding. "These strategies might help me manage my team better. I am facing similar challenges at work." Indra wondered what made opening to OG so easy.

"I know exactly what you mean," Indra saw OG still typing something out and waited patiently. "The 4 Cs aren't something you just read about—they're principles you practice. This Philosophy has been transformational for many leaders who embraced it and those they led. I'd be happy to share this magical tool kit with you."

"Oh, that would be wonderful. Thank you!" Indra replied, feeling genuinely grateful. "But," OG added, "there is a price to pay."

"Of course, "Indra muttered aloud. So, this is some commercial gimmick. She did not get that feeling from OG when they met. "She seemed so caring and a go-giver." Indra thought, suddenly feeling less warm towards OG. "Sure. What are the fees for enrolling in a course? I'm unsure if I have the time, but I can surely consider it." She wanted to create a way out if the brochure did not appeal to her.

"Haha, no, no!" OG replied with a laughing emoji. "This isn't a commercial course, and the price will have nothing to do with money." Indra flushed with embarrassment. "Oh gosh, I'm so sorry. I didn't mean to offend you."

"Don't be so apologetic, dear," OG replied warmly. "The price is the amount of time you must invest. That's a commodity more unaffordable these days, Indra." OG replied. "I share one of the 4 Cs with you during one-on-one discussions that will take 1-1.5 hours. You'll have a week to practice it and reflect on your learning. We move to the next only after demonstrating a solid understanding of the earlier C. If you skip practice in the following week, we stop. Deal?"

Indra stared at her phone, considering the commitment. With everything already on her plate—work, family, and the mounting pressure to prove herself—could she take on something this demanding? But Indra knew she needed something solid to make an impact. Before she could second-guess herself, she found her fingers typing, ""Yes, done. When do we start?" OG responded almost immediately: "Tomorrow at 3 P.M., if you're free. I'll need at least two hours for a face-to-face conversation."

Indra thought for a moment. Akhil would be taking Rhea to a friend's birthday party, and Ma was meeting her cousin. It was perfect timing. "Tomorrow works. We will meet again!"

THE POTTERY STUDIO

Around 3 P.M., Indra stood at the entrance of a pottery studio. "What an odd place for a coaching session. The studio was quiet at that hour. A few people were at the wheel, working passionately on their creations. On one side, all shapes and sizes of clay pots lined up on a shelf. Soft music played in the background, and a faint, earthy scent of wet clay filled the air.

Indra quickly saw OG at one of the potter's wheels at the studio's far end. She was being guided by a young man who instructed her from time to time on how to mould the clay and move her hands swiftly as the squashing, slapping, and silent whirl of the wheel continued.

"Welcome, Indra," OG called out when she noticed her. "Indra sat down quietly as she watched the clay take shape. OG worked patiently, pausing now and then to adjust the curve or smooth the edges. OG stopped the wheel in a few moments and skilfully picked the piece using a thread. She set it aside on a table, cleaned her hands, and joined Indra.

"Do you visit the studio regularly?" Indra asked, breaking the silence. "I try to come at least once every fifteen days,"

OG replied, smiling. It's my happy place. I find peace here. It's where I reflect, create, and let my mind wander."

Then, OG gestured towards her day's work and asked, "You see this?" She asked. "This started a lump of clay. It turned into something beautiful with time, attention, and care." And then suddenly, out of nowhere, the next question came like a bolt of lightning" "Tell me, Indra—why do you want to lead your team? What's your why?" Indra blinked, caught off guard. "What do you mean?"

"Think of leadership as this lump of clay," OG explained, pointing to the wheel. "It's messy, challenging, and requires constant effort. But it is easy to give up unless you are clear about what you want to create out of this lump unless you care deeply about what you are creating. So, tell me, what is your deeper reason for stepping into this role? What drives you?"

The room fell silent as OG's words settled in. Indra glanced at the potter's wheel, looked at the lump of clay lying close to her, and felt the question's weight. Absentmindedly, she picked the clay and started playing with it.

"Take your time," OG added gently. "Leadership isn't about power or position. It is about creating something meaningful. If you can't answer your why, the challenges will feel heavier than they are."

She quoted Stephen R. Covey: "If the ladder is not leaning against the right wall, every step we take just gets us to the wrong place faster."

THE WHY BEHIND THE WHAT

"Why do I want to lead?" she repeated softly. She pressed her palms into the clay. Her throat tightened, her lips quivered, and her fingers trembled as she shaped it. "Because my organization has given me the opportunity," she muttered unconvincingly.

Ojaswi smiled, her eyes transfixed on Indra. "Is that it?" she asked gently. And the two women became quiet. For Indra, the silence was screaming, challenging her to find out why.

"Perhaps not." Indra's voice grew softer, her vulnerability creeping in. After a long pause, she finally said, "I want to lead because I WANT TO. Because I'm worth it. That's why."

She paused and looked at the clay again. "But I think I'm losing this battle, Ojaswi," she said, her voice cracking as tears rose. "Everything feels like it's slipping away. I'm becoming this ill-tempered mother—I snap at Rhea for no reason. Ma keeps helping me, but I barely acknowledge her efforts. And Akhil... I don't even know how he puts up with me. I'm impatient, distant, and... unkind."

OG's eyes softened as she leaned in slightly, letting Indra continue.

"At work, it's worse," Indra said, her voice trembling. "I have no control over Rajiv and how he cold shoulders me. Suresh constantly reminds me that I must be eternally indebted to him, and Ajay stands by and watches while I drown. The women on my team are getting marginalized. They are looking up to me to make amends for them. But here I am, struggling to establish my own identity. I feel like an utter failure. I have let everyone down, OG, including myself."

OG reached out, her hand resting gently on Indra's arm. "Indra," she said, calm yet firm, "You are in this position because you deserve to be here. Sure, you are struggling. But leading does not mean being perfect or having all the answers simultaneously. It is not a destination, Indra; it is a journey."

Indra chuckled, her hands falling limp in her lap. "I don't even know where to start." "You start," OG said with a small smile, "By having a nice Honey Ginger Lemon Tea." With that, OG led them to a small, cozy café in the courtyard, where they settled into a quiet corner table by the window. As usual, OG ordered for them. "Do you see that vase?" OG asked? Indra followed OG's gaze and nodded. "Yeh, it is so oddly shaped," Indra noted. "Yet it looks so pretty. The odd shape itself seems to be its beauty, its USP." Indra seemed amused.

"Exactly," OG's eyes twinkled as she spoke. "It may not be conventionally fitting the mark of a vase. In that sense, it is not perfect. But what is perfect, Indra? Look at the vase; it is relevant and serves the purpose of what it is made for. And yet, it does not fit the norm. IT is the norm. When you look at rows and rows of vases, it stands out. Because it is unique, diverse."

"You're like that vase, Indra," OG said softly. "Your leadership doesn't have to fit the prototype. It does not even have to be flawless. It must be intentional. It must stand for what you believe is leadership. It must be authentic. And it should come from within."

Indra stared into her cup, her soul soaking every word uttered by OG.

OG continued, "I want you to sit with this question: What do you truly want? Not what the organization wants or what Suresh, Rajiv, or anyone else expects. What does Indra want? Because only when you know your answer can you start shaping something meaningful—like that vase out there."

Indra nodded slowly, her mind spinning but her heart feeling slightly lighter.

"And the 4 Cs can be a great Philosophical foundation for building this mansion. "OG was firm and confident, yet not pushy. "There's no rush, Indra. If you're not ready, we can start with the first C whenever you feel up to it."

Indra shook her head, her resolve becoming stronger. She set her cup down. "No, OG, I'm ready," she said firmly, her eyes glistening with determination. "I feel there's no better time than now. I want to carve a way for myself and pave the way for others. I want to share my experiences during the WIN moments of the Listening Circle. I want to back myself, to be my support, and to be the voice of other women in my team." Indra suddenly felt the calm she had been searching for weeks. It was as if the sun was finally breaking through the thick clouds, ready to illuminate her path.

THE FIRST C

OG leaned back in her chair, her gaze thoughtful. "The first C is Conscious Curiosity, Indra."

"Let me explain it this way—imagine you are holding a prism. When light passes through it, you see a spectrum of colours. Now, think of Consciousness as a point where the light bends and splits into rainbow colours. "OG picked up a tissue and drew a prism and the refraction of light as she spoke.

Indra listened intently, not sure where they were headed. "For humans, it is a space of Consciousness, an awareness that helps us fully understand our being and how it impacts our surroundings. It is about understanding the thoughts, emotions, and behaviours—in yourself and others. It's being aware of how you show up in the world and how it responds to you."

She paused for a moment, letting the metaphor sink in. OG continued, "Now, Curiosity is like tilting the prism ever so slightly to go beyond what meets the eye. It is that inquisitiveness to explore perspectives and find an answer to the "why." Why do I react the way I do? Why do people see things the way they do, and what shapes their reactions?"

"Conscious Curiosity is about combining self-awareness with a genuine desire to learn more about self and others—not to judge or fix, but to understand," OG concluded a long but profound monologue.

Indra frowned, leaning back in her chair. "It sounds... poetic. But how does that help me in real life? Rajiv has a condescending attitude 24 by 7. Suresh practically gloats about how he 'gave' me this position. And my boss, Ajay, has a wall of China built between us that I cannot surmount, at least in this lifetime. Knowing why they do what they do doesn't change the fact that they're making my life miserable."

OG sat silently, a gentle smile on her face. She looked at Indra and insisted, "You're right. Understanding them will not change their behaviour. But it will change your ability to deal with them. And that is where your power lies. Tell me, Indra, how do you feel when Rajiv undermines you? What is your immediate reaction?"

Indra sighed, tired and frustrated, "Ohh, internally, I feel like punching and hurling him out of the boxing ring. But outwardly, I try to hide my anger. I either push back, which worsens things, or I stay quiet and seethe about it later. But I surely become very defensive," Indra sighed.

OG tilted her head. "And in those moments, are you aware of how you come across? Your tone, your body language, your expressions?"

Indra hesitated, her brows furrowing. "I guess...sometimes... or... "she murmured, "Not really. I'm too caught up in the moment." She finally admitted.

"Exactly," OG said gently. That's where Consciousness comes in. You react instinctively without knowing how your emotions drive your tone, words, and posture. And here's the thing—your reactions shape how others perceive you. Rajiv is enjoying that he is having this effect on you. Your team members see that they can push your buttons quickly. Your stakeholders pick up on your defensiveness, frustration, and exhaustion."

"But Conscious Curiosity helps you to look at yourself and the surroundings in slow motion. It helps you to reflect. What's happening within me? How is it showing up in my behaviour? How might that behaviour impact others? It's about becoming aware of your light as it hits the prism and making sense of the dispersion while it is happening."

Indra leaned forward now, her tone defensive but tinged with curiosity. "But what about the others? Rajiv's arrogance, Suresh's patronizing tone—shouldn't they be the ones reflecting on their behaviour?"

"Of course," OG said, nodding. "But that is their choice. You can only have a say in the dispersion of your light, Indra. You can regulate your emotions, how you show up, and how you handle those situations."

Indra looked down at her honey ginger tea, her fingers tracing the cup's rim. "I don't know if I can do that. I have spent so long reacting—how do I... stop?"

OG paused, sensing Indra's resistance. She gestured to the pottery studio behind them. They could see a potter working on a vase across the window, her hands wet with clay. "Look at her," OG said softly. They saw the potter picking up the clay off the wheel and starting again. "That potter knows precisely what she wants to create. But the clay doesn't always cooperate. Sometimes it's too soft; sometimes it's too dry. She doesn't get frustrated or give up. She stays curious. She feels the clay, assesses its merits, and then moulds it as needed. Conscious Curiosity is like that."

But Indra sat there with her arms crossed, skepticism etched in her face. "So, you're telling me when Rajiv behaves like a bully, I step back and ask myself, why is he doing this? What does it say about him? What does it say about me?" She rolled her eyes and waved her hands in the air in frustration. "And what if it just proves that Rajiv is a jerk?" she said with raised bros and a dry voice.

A small smile tugged at the corner of OG's lips. "Even then, the clarity you gain is invaluable. Imagine this—if you understand that his behaviour comes from insecurity or fear, it stops being about you. You realize it's his struggle, not yours. That understanding frees you. "Conscious Curiosity doesn't mean you let people walk all over you. It means you choose your battles wisely and fight them strategically." OG concluded. Indra stayed quiet, staring into her tea.

"I get what you are saying, OG. I am just not sure if I can practice it." Indra seemed lost. "But I want to give this a shot. Alright, let's do this." Indra nodded slowly, a tiny flicker of determination in her eyes.

THE CONSCIOUS CURIOSITY QUADRANT

"So, are we ready to dive in?" OG asked.

"Dive into what?" Indra seemed surprised.

"We have not started exploring Conscious Curiosity fully, my dear." OG smiled. "This is the starting line of this journey. If you take the first step and cross this line, you are bound by the promise to give this a shot and find ways of practicing this for a week. So, are you ready to commit?"

Indra hesitated for a moment. But responded firmly and sincerely, "Yes, ma'am. I am all set to own my prism." She said enthusiastically.

"Alright, in that case, here we go." OG reached for her beautifully handcrafted cotton bag and brought a laminated card. It looked like a two-by-two matrix with some words printed on it.

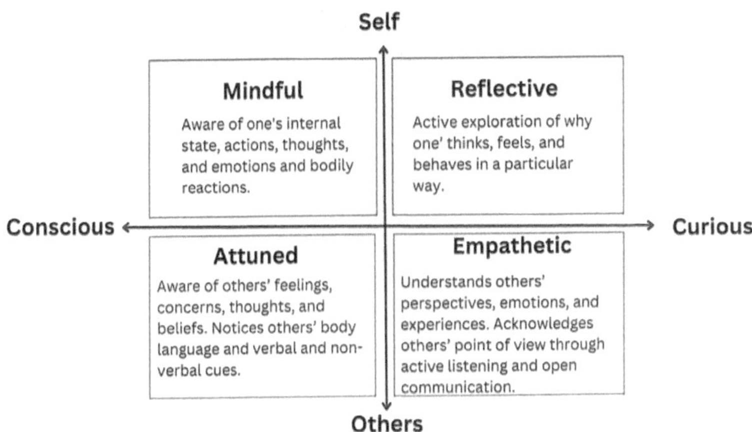

"So, here's how this framework looks. Conscious vs Curious on one axis and Self vs Others on the other." OG crossed the lines of the quadrant with her fingers. "Let's break them down together. Ready?"

Indra suddenly felt unsure about the whole thing. She nodded hesitantly. I'm ready to listen... but I'm unsure how this will help with everything I'm juggling."

OG seemed unfazed. She was not allowing Indra to look back now. "Fair point. Let's explore it using examples from your work. The first quadrant is:

Conscious Self, Let's call it being MINDFUL.

"Being mindful of what is happening within us and how it is seen on the outside. Indra, can you imagine a recent moment when you felt like your emotions took over?"

Indra thought momentarily and then said, "Last Wednesday, Rajiv interrupted me during the meeting again. I just lost it; I snapped at him. The room went quiet, and I felt... like an idiot."

OG's eyes lit up. "That's a good example. What were you feeling at that moment?" Indra paused, "Frustration, anger... I think it was more like helplessness. It felt like he was undermining me in front of everyone." she said, slowly looking up to OG for help.

OG continued to probe, "And how do you think these emotions showed up in your tone, your body language?". Indra sighed, "I raised my voice. I didn't even realize I'd slammed my pen down until afterward."

OG's eyes lit up. "That's what being 'Mindful' is about—pausing to notice those emotions and our actions.

Then she continued. "Now, let's move to quadrant two:

Curious about Self, Let's call it being Reflective.

"This is where you question your assumptions and motivations." OG was enjoying her moment with the model. "Let me ask you this: Why do you think Rajiv gets under your skin so much?" Indra frowned, "I... I think it's because he reminds me of all the people who have made me feel inferior. It's like a trigger." Suddenly, Indra seemed embarrassed.

"In its true sense, nobody can make you feel inferior. So, what do you tell yourself about him? What makes you feel so?" OG paused.

Indra was reflecting deeply. "Perhaps I have to prove myself, and the fact that he undermines me shows that I may not be good enough, and I can't allow him to ruin my reputation?" she said softly. Something in her seemed to move.

OG acknowledged, "That's a powerful insight. Curious Self is about digging into those triggers and asking, 'Why am I reacting this way? Is there another way to see this situation?"

Indra was pensive. "So, it's not just about what I see in my behaviour—it's also about what's beneath, thoughts, beliefs and fears." Indra was thinking aloud, gazing out the window, and figuring out the quadrants in her head. OG did not want Indra to drown in her thoughts yet. "Let's move to the next quadrant:

Conscious of Others, Let's call it Being Attuned.

"When Ajay stays indifferent during meetings, what do you notice about him?" Indra frowned. "He tends to lean back, arms crossed, as if he's already uninterested. And the rest of the team… they go quiet."

OG was impressed. "That's a keen observation. Being 'Attuned' is about going deeper. What are people communicating? What is impacting peoples' interaction? It is a keen observer. When you're conscious of others, you not only notice their behaviours but also think about their emotions and motivations."

She continued," "Now, let's move to the last quadrant

Curious about Others, Let's call it being Empathetic. "Here, you actively seek to understand others' perspectives. Let's go back to Rajiv. When he challenges your decisions, what is your usual reaction?"

Without wasting a moment, Indra blurted, "I try to shut him down. He's so condescending, it irritates me." She said, rolling her eyes. OG could not resist a smile, "What if, instead of shutting him down, you got curious? What if you acknowledge, 'Rajiv, I hear your concern. Can you walk me through your reasoning?'" Indra became quiet. "How do you think that would play out?" OG enquired.

"He might feel heard. Maybe he wouldn't be so combative next time." Indra was unsure but thinking.

OG smiled, "Exactly. Curiosity invites dialogue. It helps you move from confrontation to collaboration." She sat in silence, letting Indra soak the model. Then she said. "Now, let's make it real." She was not ready to let go of Indra just yet. "Think about a situation from work where you can practice each quadrant."

Indra began to enjoy this mental sprint; she said thoughtfully, "I could observe his reactions more closely in meetings, trying to understand what's driving his dismissiveness."

OG triumphed, "Great." And with Rajiv, how can you practice Empathy?"

"Oh, do I have to? "Indra gave a fake groan. She smiled, "I could start by giving him a kinder look. "She continued to mull over the thought and said, "I can ask him questions instead of jumping to conclusions."

OG seemed impressed. "Perfect. And for Mindfulness, maybe reflect on how your tone comes across in those moments. Lastly, Reflection—what is one assumption about yourself you would like to challenge this week?" Indra paused, "Maybe I need to have all the answers all the time. I think that's why I get defensive, "she said after a couple of minutes of thinking.

The framework felt less abstract now—something tangible, a lens Indra could apply to daily challenges. With OG's gentle guidance, she began to see how Conscious Curiosity could be her ally on this journey.

THE JOURNAL

It was almost 4:30 P.M. Indra could not believe they had spoken for almost 1.5 hours. "It is so easy to be around OG," Indra thought. I wish I could be like her…. Someday…"

While Indra was reflecting on their conversation, OG again picked up her bag, removed a beautiful blue book, and handed it to Indra. Indra took it with a confused look, "What's this?" Oh, it is a journal," Indra smiled. I love journals. I used to write regularly in the past… But now, I don't remember when I picked up a pen last… ""Now you will," OG smiled. "Part of the deal is to do homework and practice what we discuss." Indra's face looked worried. "Ahh, the homework," she repeated, shuffling through the journal pages.

"Your task is to spend 10-15 minutes each day noting down anything that you observed, reflected on, or processed through the day related to the first C. At the end of the week, you write an insight summary and send me an image." OG turned the pages and stopped to point out the page. "If you are serious about this journey, you will be diligent about your homework, and we will make our next appointment," OG said matter-of-factly without any air of authority or threat. Interestingly, Indra was more excited than worried. "Let's go girl…" Indra said aloud, hugged OG, and left.

SMALL CHANGE

Monday morning brought with it the urgency of another workweek. Indra sat at her desk, sipping her lukewarm coffee, her calendar glaring back at her like an unsympathetic taskmaster. Two critical meetings dominated her day—the first with her team to strategize for the Project Zenit launch and, later, a review with the senior leadership team on ProMax. She took a deep breath and braced herself for the day.

A strong cologne aroma hit her as she entered her team meeting room. The projector was on, softly casting a bluish glow on the wall. Her team members were already seated, laptops open, eyes fixed on their screens, and each entirely oblivious to others in the room.

"Good morning, everyone." Indra started on a high note. After a few mumbles and non-verbal acknowledgments, the meeting began. "Alright, let's get started, Aditi. Please help us understand the product features your team is proposing for Zenith. "Indra was ready to take notes.

Aditi began presenting her ideas. Her voice was steady, but Indra noticed a slight quiver at the edges—a hesitation that betrayed her nervousness. While Aditi explained the features, Rajiv sat in his chair, typing furiously on the keyboard of his laptop. The clicking of his keys was annoying, and Aditi was trying hard not to get distracted by the noise.

Before Indra could call out Rajiv's behaviour, Naveen cut Aditi out. "What's the data to back this up?" he asked sharply, leaning forward with an arched brow. Before Aditi could respond, Rajiv smirked and muttered, "Data seems optional these days."

The comment, meant as a joke, landed with the weight of a punch. Aditi's cheeks flushed, and her hands tightened around the edges of her notebook. Indra saw it all—Aditi's shoulders slumped slightly, and her voice lost its earlier conviction. Indra's instinct was to step in and shield Aditi from her colleagues' condescending attacks, but she hesitated momentarily. Aditi ignored the comments and summed up her presentation, her tone flatter now. She finished quickly, leaving an uneasy silence in her wake.

The meeting dragged on for another twenty minutes, but Indra realized she had failed to intervene. She could feel her cheeks flushing and her body getting tense. She clenched her fists briefly, frustration bubbling under the surface. Why didn't I do more? Why didn't I say something to make her feel safe?

The morning experience had left her conscious about what had happened. In a fragile state, she returned to her desk and opened the presentation for the board meeting. She had shared the draft with Ajay earlier, hoping for his insights, but there were none. She picked up her phone and dialled his number. "Ajay, did you get to look at the deck?" she asked.

"Yeah, looks fine," he replied casually.

"Do you have any suggestions? Should I add more details on how we are ramping up the security checks?"

"OK. Whatever you feel," Ajay said, his tone indifferent.

A hot wave of anger surged within Indra. She felt the muscles in her jaw tighten. Why does he always steer away from getting involved? She was about to snap but paused instead, taking a deep breath. Mindfulness and Reflection, she reminded herself. She closed her eyes briefly, grounding herself.

"Ajay, can I ask you something?" she said, her voice softer now. "Sure," he replied, a hint of curiosity in his tone.

"I've noticed you don't intervene when I struggle to put forth our stand as a team during meetings or discussions. Sometimes, it feels like you're not entirely with me on things. Am I imagining it?"

There was a pause on the line. "Hello, Ajay." She wondered if Ajay had dropped off. "Yes, I am here, Indra. "She waited patiently. "It's not that, Indra," Ajay said, his voice quieter than before. "I just... I don't want to micromanage and contribute without a reason."

She could hear the shift in his tone—less defensive, more thoughtful. She didn't push further. Let's leave it at that, she told herself. "I respect you for the vast experience you bring in Ajay, and I want to learn from you. Any suggestion you give, even review comments on my work, will be most helpful." She decided not to push the topic further.

"OK," was all Ajay said.

The board meeting that afternoon carried its usual air of formality. The meeting progressed as expected, with Suresh setting the context, Indra presenting their view and data, and Ravindran, the Sales head, sharing some more insights they picked from the client. The meeting was uneventful.

Interestingly, Indra noticed Ajay was more engaged than she had seen in a long time. He responded to a couple of questions confidently and even backed her up when one of the board members raised a concern about timelines.

As the meeting wrapped up, Indra found herself reflecting on the day. Was Ajay's shift in behaviour a result of their earlier conversation? Or was she imagining things through the lens of her newfound focus on Conscious Curiosity?

Either way, something felt different. Small, yes, but different. And for the first time in weeks, she felt a flicker of hope.

Life is like an ever-shifting kaleidoscope—a slight change and all patterns alter. Indra was reminded of a quote by Sharon Salzberg from her book Loving Kindness: The Revolutionary Art of Happiness.

A CAFETERIA CONVERSATION

The week was a blur of deadlines, meetings, and pressure. Between the demands of ProMax and the Project Zenith launch, Indra had too many balls in the air. On Wednesday, by afternoon, she was exhausted. Her head ached, and she was tired of the constant back-and-forth with the RFP team. Her eyes watered from endless pouring through data sheets and Excel spreadsheets.

"I need a break," she thought, heading toward the cafeteria.

The cafeteria was always a riot of colours, aroma, and life energy. Indra had done some of her best thinking and writing in the cafeteria. The aroma of freshly baked veg puffs was irresistible. Indra picked one puff and some coffee and started scouting for a vacant table. Just then, she spotted Sneha at a nearby table. Sneha sat alone, scrolling on her phone. The sun rays streaming through the French window just about fell on her, making her hair shine and face glow.

"Hi there!" Indra called out, her voice carrying a hint of cheer despite her fatigue. She walked over, hoping to share a light, informal chat. Sneha looked up, hesitated for a moment, then smiled faintly. "Hi, Indra." "Mind if I join you?" Indra asked, pulling out a chair before Sneha could answer. "Sure," Sneha said, her tone measured.

Indra leaned forward slightly, placed her tray on the table, and settled. She noticed that Sneha was having a salad. "I envy those who are disciplined eaters." Indra started in a non-threatening way. Sneha loosened a bit. "It's rare for me to choose a salad." She smiled sheepishly. "Most times, I also sit on the same side as you do." Sneha grinned.

Encouraged by this response, Indra asked, "How's everything going? "She kept her voice casual but curious. Sneha hesitated, her fingers fidgeting with the edge of her phone case. "Fine," she said, but her tone lacked conviction.

Indra noticed that their space was filled with unspoken words. Her chest tightened slightly, a familiar discomfort that came when she sensed things were not as smooth as they appeared. "Stay open. Stay curious," she reminded herself.

Indra pressed gently, keeping her tone warm. "I've always appreciated how you speak your mind, Sneha. You are sharp and observant. If there's something I should know, I'm open to hearing it."

Sneha paused and hesitated a bit and then gave a long sigh. She set her phone down and spoke. "Well, since you asked, I do have some concerns." Indra felt her body tense, and her grip on the mug tightened slightly. She wanted to run for cover, not sure what to expect, but she continued to lean back in her chair and encouraged Sneha to continue. "Go on," she said.

Sneha hesitated again and deliberately said, "Indra, you're not doing justice to us." Indra froze. She had not expected such a blunt response. Sneha continued, her voice gaining confidence. "You're letting certain behaviours slide. Some senior guys—the so-called oldies—act like it's their birthright to dominate every conversation and every decision. It's making some of us feel... invisible." Indra was quiet and urged Sneha to go on.

Sneha leaned forward slightly, her voice dropping. "Remember the team sync last week? We were discussing the marketing strategy for Zenith, and Ankit, my intern, suggested a different approach for targeting younger audiences through social media influencers. He barely finished two sentences before Rajiv cut him off, saying it was a waste of time. 'Let's stick to traditional channels,' he said, and nobody, including you, challenged him. Ankit just went quiet after that. His idea had merit, Indra, but it never stood a chance." Indra could see the incident clearly in her mind's eye.

Sneha wasn't done. "And then there was the review meeting last week. Priya presented her analysis of the pre-sales issues. She had put in hours, but Naveen openly laughed at one of her slides, calling it 'amateurish.' Priya barely spoke for the rest of the meeting. Do you know she sat through two presentations without uttering a word after that meeting?"

Indra was shocked to realize that she had no recollection of this event. She was not conscious of what was happening around her. Her throat tightened, her mind racing with justifications she could offer. But instead, Indra took a deep breath, letting the words settle.

"Thank you for sharing this, Sneha," she said after a moment. Her voice was steady, but she could feel the weight of the conversation pressing down on her. "It is not easy to be candid without worrying about the impact, and I assure you I will be vigilant about such incidents going forward."

Sneha seemed to relax a bit, her shoulders easing as she leaned back in her chair. "I know it's not easy to digest such feedback. I appreciate you asking and being OK with my bluntness," Sneha said. I also know you care. That's why I wanted to bring it up." Indra nodded, her gaze fixed on the table momentarily before meeting Sneha's eyes again. "You're right. I've been so caught up in everything else that I haven't paid enough attention to these dynamics. I need to do better—for you, the team, and myself."

Sneha smiled faintly. "I appreciate that, Indra. I really do. And I'm here to support you in any way I can." As Sneha stood to leave, she paused and turned back. "Thanks for listening. It means a lot." Indra watched her walk away, leaving behind a trail of emotions for her to manage—guilt, disappointment, and pride—pride that she had stayed open, curious, and conscious of her reactions. Her journey was far from over, but today felt like a small, meaningful step in the right direction. She had some thoughts to share with her journal. She smiled.

THE RHYTHM OF FRIDAY NIGHTS

Friday nights were Indra's favourite. They gave a feeling of abundance, given that there were two full days ahead where Indra could choose her pace. After dinner, everyone was relaxing in the drawing room. Rhea sat in the corner cross-legged on the floor, carefully cutting and pasting colourful paper to create a greeting card for her best friend. The steady snip of scissors and the rustling of paper filled the air. Across the room, Ma was engrossed reading a book, her reading glasses perched on her nose. The steady hum of the rocking chair filled the room.

Indra was quite pleased with her progress on the first C.

"Homework is done, ma.am." She had texted OG and sent her the summary picture. Indra leaned back on the couch, a satisfied smile on her lips. She glanced at her phone, re-reading the message she had sent earlier to OG:

"Homework done, ma'am." The text was accompanied by a snapshot of her notes and a summary of her reflections on the first C—Consciousness and Curiosity.

"Well done, Indra! The first step is always the hardest. We will befriend the second C tomorrow."

Indra was looking forward to meeting OG the next day at 11 A.M. "What would be revealed tomorrow?" she wondered.

FIRST C- MY INSIGHTS
Consciousness and Curiosity

MINDFULNESS

- I realized that my silence in meetings isn't neutral—it sends a message. Inaction can inadvertently reinforce negative behaviors.

  - During the meeting, I did not call out dismissive remarks and interruption by others. That left Aditi deflated

- By becoming aware of my emotions, I could redirect my frustration with Ajay into a constructive dialogue, which shifted his engagement.

REFLECTION

- Reflecting on Sneha's feedback helped me realize how unchecked behaviors had affected team morale and silenced younger voices.

- My own body language and tone often mirror my emotions, and I've learned to reflect on their unspoken impact on others.

EMPATHETIC EXPLORATION

- Seeking to understand others' experiences rather than justify my own actions has opened doors for honest feedback and trust.

  - I explored Ajay's disengagement by genuinely inquiring about his perspective, which led to a surprising shift in his participation.

ATTUNEMENT

- Being attuned to non-verbal cues helps me navigate delicate situations with greater precision.

- During the board meeting, Ajay's body language softened after our earlier discussion, signaling a subtle but positive change in our dynamic.

STORM BEFORE THE CALM

While Indra put her phone down, she heard Akhil speak casually while watching the news channel., "Hey Indra, I won't be home tomorrow," The approaching storm challenged Indra's peace. "Oh," Indra muttered, her disappointment hanging like a heavy curtain.

Akhil turned to look at her, frowning. "What was that supposed to mean?" "Nothing," Indra replied, trying to keep her tone neutral, though the irritation was unmistakable in her voice. "Nothing, huh?" Akhil pressed, his annoyance visible. "Indra, what is it?"

"Akhil, I said it's nothing. Why are you making a big deal out of this?" Her voice wavered, and the tension in the room thickened by the second. Akhil abruptly turned off the TV. The sudden silence was deafening. "Indra, there you go again. Your regular pattern."

"Pattern? What pattern?" Indra shot back, her voice now edged with anger. She could feel her cheeks flush, her body tightening with frustration. "Don't act like you don't know," Akhil retorted, his voice rising. "I've been around all the time for Rhea.

And the one day I want some time for myself, all I get from you is an 'Oh'?!"

"Akhil, I haven't even complained! Have I said a single word?" Indra felt her control slip, and her voice grew louder. "You don't need to, Indra!" Akhil cut her off, his words sharp. "Your body language says it all." He stormed out of the room, leaving Indra stunned and trembling.

The silence that followed was suffocating. Rhea had stopped pasting and was staring at her parents, wide-eyed, the half-cut papers flying around her. Ma had put down her book and was sitting still, looking visibly disturbed.

"Beta," Ma began hesitantly. He does so much for the family; how can you be so…." Her voice trailed off. "How can I be what, Ma? Say it—selfish? Is that what you think?" Indra's voice cracked, tears threatening to spill.

"I am grateful for everything Akhil does and for you too. I really am. But am I wrong to feel upset when there's no heads-up? I have an important meeting Tomorrow with OG, and I told him about it four days ago. He had agreed. And now, he declares he can't be there. How is that fair? And all of this over a single 'Oh'?" Her words echoed in the room. Ma looked away, clearly uncomfortable, and Rhea quietly returned to her greeting card, though her work was now hurried and uneven. And then it dawned upon Indra.

Consciousness and Curiosity. It wasn't just about work, was it? She could have handled Akhil much better. She could have been more conscious of her feelings and frustration. She could have probed what made Akhil say what he said. She could have been more patient and tolerant with him, just as she had been with Sneha and Ajay. Consciousness and Curiosity were ways of being—a way to navigate life's conflicts with clarity and empathy. And she had failed right here in her own home.

Indra regained her composure and texted OG.

"Hey, OG," she began, her voice calmer now. "I'm sorry, but I can't make it Tomorrow. Something's come up, and Akhil won't be able to care for things at home."

"Oh," OG texted. "No worries. I had something on Sunday, but does Sunday work for you?" "No, OG, I can't make you lose your Sunday every time," Indra replied, guilt creeping into her tone.

"Don't worry about me," OG said with her usual warmth. "In fact, I have a better idea. Why don't you join me at an event at 3.00 P.M. on Sunday? We can have high tea, and then you plan to catch up with Akhil and Rhea for an evening activity."

Indra felt her shoulders relax. "Sure. Thank you so much for accommodating, OG."

"Hey, no problem, Indra. I just loved how you noted your insights on the first C," OG added admiringly.

"Thanks, OG. See you on Sunday then."

BREAKTHROUGH

THE AIKIDO DEMO: GRACE MEETS POWER

The Friday confrontation with Akhil had left Indra emotionally raw. The weekend brought some relief, but the exchange lingered in her mind like a tangled knot in a ball of wool. After a restful day, she was eager to meet OG the following day. She couldn't help but wonder what OG had planned this time.

When Indra arrived at the Haven Wellness Studio on Sunday, she was struck by the serene atmosphere. The studio blended rustic charm with modern aesthetics—exposed wooden beams, soft lighting, and an earthy aroma of sandalwood and lemongrass. A Buddha statue was placed at the centre of a small artificial pond, water bubbling gently around the statue.

OG had asked her to come to the amphitheatre. As Indra made her way to the venue, she noticed that the studio was designed with minimalism—simple yet comfortable yellow chairs with indigo cushions. The place was full of lively plants and curios. The large windows gave the place an opulent look and flooded the area with sunlight. The amphitheatre was a modest area with a seating capacity of almost 80 people. She noticed a few rows filled with people as she entered the area. Soft murmurs, chatter, and an occasional loud laughter swept the room. She scanned the crowd, looking for OG. "Over here!" OG called, waving from a corner. Indra turned to see her mentor, dressed casually in a flowing cotton skirt and a spaghetti-strap blouse. OG's usual bold bindi was replaced by a bare, elegant look complemented by silver earrings that caught the light. "What's all this?" Indra asked, confused.

"There's an Aikido seminar and demo here," OG explained, gesturing toward the mat. "I've wanted to attend one of these for years. It won't take long—just 30 minutes. I hope you don't mind." "Aikido?" Indra frowned. "I don't know much about it."

That's OK. Watch and listen. You might learn something." OG winked as the room settled, and the demonstration began. The maestro stepped onto the mat, a woman in her sixties who moved with the grace of someone decades younger. She exuded quiet confidence, her white spotless suit and black belt tied neatly around her waist. Bowing deeply to the audience, she began to speak in a measured, soothing tone.

"Aikido is not about fighting," she explained, "It is about harmony. When an attack comes, we do not meet it with force but redirect it, neutralizing conflict without causing harm."

Two practitioners stood on the mat and bowed to each other. The demonstration began with one of the practitioners swiftly attacking the opponent. The other moved with the speed of light, ducked the attack, and redirected the motion with a spin.

Indra leaned forward, her eyes widening as the drama continued. It was like watching a dance—graceful yet potent. The moves became complex, and the intensity and engagement of the audience rose with every move. Yet the opponents seemed calm and composed. There was no trace of aggression or rage, yet each ensured the move was met with a sound deflection and redirection. The maestro narrated the techniques, urging the audience to appreciate the fine display of awareness, skill, and poise.

One practitioner tried to catch his opponent off guard in the final moments. However, the other displayed superlative awareness and control. He barely flinched, dug into a counterattack, and pinned his attacker on the ground. As the demo ended, both practitioners rose, stood facing each other, bowed, and shook hands.

The audience was thrilled and spontaneously rose to give the practitioner a standing ovation. The maestro summarized her explanation: "What you just witnessed is not a game of exercise form—it is a profound life philosophy. The Aikido practitioners don't fight back; they create a rhythm with the force and reach their goal. True strength lies in embracing reality, working with it rather than against it, and paving a path for transformation."

The demo had left the audience in awe. As the crowd dispersed, OG approached the Mastro. Indra could not hear what they spoke about but noticed that OG had handed her a file with some brochures. The maestro seemed impressed and continued to ask OG a few questions intently. Indra heard OG's final words, "I am so grateful, Maestro Akari. I hope to see you at the conference. Our budding leaders will benefit immensely from your wisdom and the Aikido Philosophy". Maestro Akari bowed, and both parted ways.

THE PREDICAMENT

As they left the studio, OG noticed Indra's subdued demeanour. "All right, what's going on?" OG asked as they stepped into the crisp morning air. Indra hesitated. The question was a gentle nudge, but it cracked open the dam she'd held back. "It's nothing and perhaps everything," Indra murmured. She shared her Friday tussle with Akhil— "Sometimes I feel nothing is worth OG." Indra seemed drained.

OG remained silent, letting Indra continue. "I feel indebted to Akhil for everything he's done for me. He believed in me when no one else did. I feel like I owe him, and because of that, I don't push back. And then I get resentful—at him, at myself. It's a mess."

OG gave her a knowing smile. "Indra, do you know what I often see happening with women in leadership or personal relationships? We hesitate to speak up or assert our needs because we feel this overwhelming sense of indebtedness. We feel grateful for every opportunity we get, as if we don't entirely deserve to be where we are. That's imposter syndrome working its magic." Indra looked up, intrigued.

"Think about it," OG continued. "How often have you thought, but for all these people, I would not have made it here, and now that I am here, I don't think I deserve to be here." Every word uttered by OG was relatable. "That mindset is common among women—whether at work or home."

Indra nodded slowly. "That's exactly how I felt on Friday. I didn't have the right to feel upset because Akhil has done so much for me and Rhea. But it didn't stop me from feeling resentful."

OG placed a hand on her shoulder. "That's where the second C comes in—Courage and Compassion. Courage to speak up, to set boundaries, to reclaim your voice. And Compassion—for yourself, for Akhil, for the situation."

Indra frowned. "Compassion? For him?"

OG smiled. "Yes. Courage without Compassion can come across as harsh or defensive. Compassion balances it. Think of Aikido—redirect the energy, don't absorb or attack it."

Indra nodded slowly. "So... I need to practice both. Courage to say what needs to be said, and Compassion to say it in a way that builds bridges, not that burns them."

OG grinned. "Exactly. More food for thought is coming your way, dear, along with actual food. Come on, let's go. Today, I will treat you with the best pizza you have ever eaten."

With OG, food was always an integral part of the meetings. As they waited for a cab to arrive, Indra added one more line to her insight note:

"Consciousness and Curiosity help us see, but Courage and Compassion help us act." "But how?" She wondered.

THE SECOND C

"Indra, during my days with this MNC, I had to engage with people of different nationalities. They would come from all over the globe: Europe, the US, and the Middle East. Do you know what I dreaded the most while interacting with them?" As they drove, OG looked out of the cab window and opened the conversation.

Indra turned towards her, raising an eyebrow. "Hmm... communicating with all the foreign delegates? Was it your accent? Or perhaps the fear of being misunderstood?" OG smiled but shook her head gently.

"No, it wasn't about communication. It was about choosing food joints for everyone." She paused for a moment, letting that sink in. "I used to get so anxious about picking a place to eat. I was most confident of my work and deliverables, but these lunches and dinners would leave me petrified. Some of these visitors were well-informed and clear on what they wanted. Some of the 'surprise me' types were the most treacherous. "Indra could not suppress a laugh, "I can't believe your biggest stressor in life was picking food. No wonder you have mastered the art after all the over-practice." Indra teased.

OG chuckled, "It was a battle between courage in making a choice based on my liking, understanding, and compassion towards their needs, preferences, and capabilities to digest our kind of food."

"Hmm, Courage and Compassion sound like a good pair. But they seem a bit dramatic in the given situation." Indra made a face.

"Maybe. But those days taught me a lot about empathy, putting oneself in others' shoes, asking versus assuming, and finally showing the Courage to stand for something you believe in. It also taught me to be OK if the other person did not reciprocate as I anticipated. It taught me to respect other people's reactions and not judge myself on the outcomes we had co-created. If they liked the food joint, that would be great news. If they did not, I would not crucify myself. Courage and Compassion keep you engaged in the process but help you distance from the obsession of a perfect outcome."

Indra sat back, processing OG's words. Her example was simple, but the underlying thought was profound.

COURAGE AND COMPASSION

The aroma of freshly baked pizzas and garlic bread filled the air as they entered Pizza Fresca. Indra sat across from OG in a cozy corner of her favourite pizzeria. Today, OG picked an Exotic Vegetable Pizza and cheese garlic bread. Absentmindedly, OG picked the garlic bread. "You know, Indra, Courage, and Compassion are like the two wings of leadership. You can't fly high unless both have good strength."

Indra looked up; her curiosity momentarily peaked. "Wings? Sounds poetic, OG, but what does it mean?"

OG leaned back, swirling her peach iced tea. "Courage is about taking bold action, standing up when it's easier to sit down. Compassion is understanding, listening, and caring for the people you lead."

OG continued, "Courage and Compassion lead to four kinds of leaders." And she brought out a card.

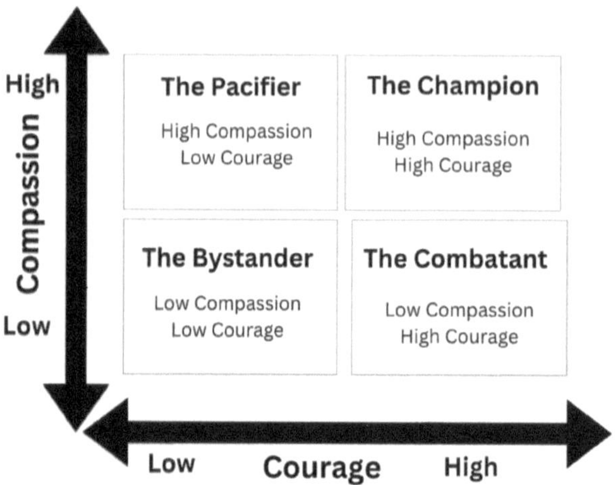

"Let's start with the first. Have you ever had a leader who let you down? Someone who didn't stand up for you when it mattered?"

Indra sighed. She didn't need to think long. "Shankar. My manager, whom I reported to two years ago. I worked on a massive project; I burnt the candle at both ends and delivered good results. Despite that, I was given a poor performance grade. When I went to him for support, he just... avoided the issue. He did not defend me, did not even try. He was always nice in meetings but disappeared when I needed him to take a stand."

OG nodded knowingly. "That's the Bystander. Low Courage, Low Compassion. They avoid action, stay passive, and let things fall apart when the moment calls for boldness. That's such a shame, isn't it?"

Indra sighed. "Yeh, they are such wasted leaders," Indra commented, her voice tightening.

OG looked at her pizza, paused to bite, and continued, "Let's flip that. Have you ever had a very caring leader who did not have the spine to support you?"

Indra frowned, thinking back. Then it hit her: "When I announced my pregnancy at work, I was due for a promotion. Ritesh, my manager, was a very kind person. He was very happy for me and clarified that I could avail myself of whatever flexi-policies I wanted. However, during the promotion discussion, he did not take a stand. Ritesh's boss felt that the time was not right for me to get a promotion, and Ritesh joined the chorus. Later, he confessed that he felt terrible for me, but ' perhaps this is the best thing for you, Indra. "You can now wholeheartedly focus on your baby and your health," were his consoling words. I felt belittled and berated."

"Hm, that's a classic Pacifier- Low Courage, High Compassion," OG explained. "They'll hold your hand through tough times but won't turn the tide for you. They're like a light blanket—comforting but not enough to protect you from strong winds."

"Now, let's get to the opposite. Ever had a leader who was bold but lacked empathy?" OG enquired.

Indra hesitated. "Not directly, but I've seen it. Rachel is a senior manager in the finance department. She's tough as a rock and never hesitates to make hard decisions, but she's... cold. She always insists that if she had to struggle, why should other women expect anything different? There are no exceptions or allowances for women juggling many responsibilities."

OG leaned forward; her tone serious. "That's The Combatant- High Courage, Low Compassion. They are no-nonsense, usually high achievers, and very hard on themselves and those around them. Organizations recognize them for their go-getter attitude, yet they do not create a nurturing environment for their teams. Indra sighed. "I've seen the damage that such kind of leadership does. People admire them but don't trust them."

OG nodded. "And now, for the rarest of them all. Have you ever had a leader who balanced both Courage and Compassion?"

Indra smiled faintly. "Yes. Chandru, my first manager. I still remember this one time during a team meeting. I pitched an idea, and a male colleague—let's call him Tom—took credit for it. I was furious but didn't know how to speak up. Chandru interrupted and said, 'Actually, that was Indra's idea. Let's hear her expand on it.' He didn't just defend me; he made sure my voice was heard. I have never worked for a manager who was as fair-minded as Chandru. Candid yet caring."

OG's eyes lit up. "That's the Champion - High Courage, High Compassion. They fight for you and with you. They inspire confidence and growth by leading with both heart and spine." Indra said warmly. "I didn't realize how rare that was until now." OG leaned back, wiping her fingers with a napkin. "So, where do you think you fall on this spectrum? Have you ever been a Champion for someone?"

Indra gulped hard; She thought she would choke on her pizza slice. "Honestly? I don't know. Maybe... no, probably not. I think I've stayed in my safe zone too often." OG smiled warmly. "The fact that you're reflecting on it means you're already on the right path. Courage and Compassion aren't fixed traits. They are muscles. You need to start exercising them."

Indra sighed, but it felt lighter this time. "I'll try." "Good," OG said, raising her glass of iced tea. "Here's to not just managing but leading."

"Oh, and Indra? Courage and Compassion aren't just leadership traits. They're life traits. Don't leave them at the office." A classic OG tip lingered long after the pizza was gone.

SECOND C BEGINS AT HOME

Indra and Akhil strolled through the neighbourhood park, enjoying the cool breeze. The setting sun was painting the sky with crimson hues. Indra wore her usual casual evening attire—a simple beige kurta with delicate floral embroidery and well-fitted jeans, her hair pulled back in a neat ponytail. Akhil had his hands casually tucked into his pockets in his relaxed olive-green polo shirt and track pants.

Indra hesitated before she spoke, her tone gentle yet steady. "Akhil, I've been thinking about our conversation on Friday. I realized something about myself during that discussion—and about us." Akhil turned to look at her, curiosity flickering in his eyes. "What is it?" She hesitated momentarily and said softly, "I feel like I'm always operating from a place of indebtedness. Everyone expects me to take care of household responsibilities as my duties. However, when you or Ma contribute, it feels... like a special privilege. The feeling overwhelms me," Indra said, her voice laced with vulnerability. Akhil remained silent for a moment. Indra could not read his expression and wondered if he was offended or if he was reflecting on what she said. Finally, he sighed,

Indra smiled, feeling a wave of relief. "I'm not blaming you, Akhil. It's something we've both grown accustomed to. But it's time we looked at this differently—as partners, not just as assigned roles. I am sure you also may have your pain point. Akhil gazed at the skies and said slowly, "Not really, but sometimes I feel significantly cut off from you. I am not blaming you; I know things are tough at work. I wish we could spend time together, seeing each other's world. "Indra was touched. She held Akhil's hand and said, "Absolutely; let's try this again and make it work better."

He nodded, reaching for her hand. "Yes, let's do it. And Indru, I'm sorry for overreacting earlier." As they continued their walk, the air between them felt lighter, the unspoken barriers melting away. Indra made a mental note to document this in her diary later:

Conscious Curiosity helps you see things from different perspectives;

Courage and Compassion help you address them purposefully.

THE NEW LENS

The following week spun a series of events on Indra that gave a good understanding of the second C and an excellent opportunity to practice Courage and Compassion. This time, she made detailed notes of these instances in her journal.

Monday Morning, 9:00 A.M. – Indra's Office

Monday morning always meant a jam-packed morning, an intense afternoon, and a rushed evening. Indra glanced at her packed calendar. First on the agenda was a meeting with Vivek to review the progress of the project development team. They had to review the product development reports and devise action steps to improve their offerings.

"Good morning, Vivek," she said warmly as he walked in. He looked sharp in a checkered shirt and neatly pressed chinos, but his usual enthusiasm seemed tempered today. "Good morning, Indra," he said, settling into the chair opposite her desk. Indra leaned forward, hands clasped. "So, how are the wedding preparations coming along?" She had decided to spend a few moments connecting with her team beyond work whenever possible. Vivek sighed, absentmindedly staring at a new tattoo on his wrist. "It's going fine. Honestly, it's overwhelming at times. Everybody around us seems more excited about the event than us. Besides, my fiancée, Shuchi, is also struggling with a life-changing decision."

"I hope she is not reconsidering getting married to you." Aditi, who had just entered the room, said with a mischievous tone. "Hopefully not, "Vivek grinned. She's thinking of starting her own business because, well… later, with kids and everything, it'll be difficult. And she wants to take this plunge as a proactive step rather than start something on a knee-jerk."

Indra's eyebrows arched, her tone sharpening slightly. "Hey, isn't that a knee-jerk response? I am sure times have changed, Vivek. Today's employers are quite supportive about such things." Indra pressed on. Before Vivek could respond, Aditi jumped into the conversation. "That's nice to say and good to hear, Indra. But ground realities are different. Even our own company hasn't been particularly supportive of working mothers. I've seen it happen—women are often sidelined when they have kids. Last week, Kavya from Dave's team put in her papers because Dave was not supporting her enough."

Indra sat up in her chair. Indra had no clue what Aditi was talking about. Did Kavya need support? Dave had never mentioned this or checked with her to see if Kavya could be given extra concessions. Indra did not press the topic, but her heart sank. She believed that her workplace was progressive, but this was a blind spot she couldn't ignore. She made a mental note to take the issue up with Dave.

Monday Afternoon, 4:00 P.M. – A Chat with Saumitra

Indra's mind raced as she replayed the morning conversation. Was Dave simply a Bystander, or was he a Combatant who did not want to support Kavya? Indra found herself frequently diving into her new vocabulary. She couldn't decide, but she was determined to find out. She decided to call Saumitra.

"Hi Saumitra, got a minute to spare?" Indra checked. "I've got lots of minutes to spare," he replied cheerfully. "I have just survived a three-hour-long meeting and heading to the cafeteria for tea. Care to join?" Indra was in no mood for a coffee or a bite but seized the opportunity to spend uninterrupted time with Saumitra. "Perfect. I am just outside your office. Will be happy to join," Indra said, relieved. She preferred face-to-face conversations, especially when the topic was sensitive.

Monday Afternoon, 4:15 P.M. – The cafeteria

Saumitra and Indra went to the 5th-floor cafeteria, picked up their tea, and found a corner table. Saumitra's dark blue shirt was slightly crumpled, and his posture revealed his fatigue. "How are things going?" she asked, leaning back in her chair. "Surviving," Saumitra sighed. "The usual hue and cry over attrition rates."

Indra nodded. "Yes, that's actually why I wanted to meet you." Saumitra raised an eyebrow. "Wait, don't tell me you're resigning, Indra. You can't do that. There's too much at stake, and leaders like you can't just jump the ship." Indra laughed, shaking her head. "Relax, I'm not going anywhere. But I do need to talk about something important." Saumitra exhaled in relief. "Oh, that's OK. I'm sorry to pounce on you this way, "he said sheepishly.

Indra leaned in slightly. "Saumitra, has Kavya from Dave's team resigned?" Saumitra's face darkened. "Yes. Didn't Dave mention this to you?" Indra shook her head, her tone sharpening. "No, he didn't." Saumitra paused, choosing his words carefully.

"Kavya's son is on the autism spectrum, Indra. She's doing an incredible job managing his care. Both she and her husband take turns taking him to therapy sessions, and it's really helping him. But with the new back-to-office policy, she's finding it nearly impossible to balance everything."

Indra's expression softened, though frustration lingered beneath the surface. "But Kavya is such a valuable asset. Can't we do something to support her?"

Saumitra gave her a pointed look. "You're asking me? You're the boss here, Indra. If anyone can initiate this conversation, it's you." Indra sighed, her frustration growing. "I can't act on something I don't know about, Saumitra. Why didn't Dave bring this to my attention?" Saumitra hesitated. "Maybe he was planning to talk to you today. Kavya just put in her papers on Friday evening, and it's only Monday. He hasn't approved her resignation yet."

Indra fell silent, unconvinced. She felt a mix of disappointment and urgency. "What do you think I should do?" she asked finally. "Confront him," Saumitra said without hesitation. Indra nodded. Yes, confrontation was necessary. But she reminded herself that Compassion must always accompany Courage. And compassion wasn't just for Kavya—it had to extend to Dave as well.

Monday Evening, 4.30 P.M. - Back in Her Office

Indra sat at her desk. She picked up her pen and jotted down her thoughts, trying to organize her approach for the conversation with Dave. She decided to call Dave. "Hey Dave, do you have a minute…" "Yes, can we meet? There is something important I want to talk to you about…. Yes, my work desk, maybe 6 P.M.? OK, great. See you then."

Monday Evening, 6:00 P.M. – Indra's Office

By 6 P.M., the natural light that usually streamed through the blinds of Indra's office was gone and was replaced by the soft glow from the ceiling lights casting long shadows on the walls. Indra had just wrapped up her report for Ajay on the Project Zenith Status when she noticed Dave approaching her cabin. "Hey Dave, come on in," she waved and invited Dave.

Dave stepped in, looking slightly hesitant. He was dressed more casually than usual—a Lacoste blue polo shirt and blue jeans. His hair was quite dishevelled, and his face gave a haggard look, suggesting he had had a long day. "Hi Indra, did you want to see me?" he asked, his tone polite but guarded. "Yes, Dave. Please, have a seat," Indra gestured to the chair opposite her. She took a moment to observe his body language—the slight stiffness in his posture and the furrow in his brow.

"How's everything going with your team?" she started, her voice warm, easing him into the conversation. Dave shrugged. "It's fine. You know how it is—always something to fix."

Indra leaned forward slightly, resting her arms on her desk. "I heard Kavya put in her resignation on Friday. Is that true?" Dave blinked, clearly surprised. "Yes, that's correct. I was going to bring it up with you today."

Indra nodded; her tone measured. "Dave, I understand she's been struggling with the new back-to-work policy. Did she talk to you about it?" Dave adjusted his glasses and cleared his throat. "She mentioned that the back-to-work schedule impacts her son's therapy sessions. Indra, I want you to know that she opted to leave. I have not asked her to do that. I am just honouring her decision," Dave said defensively.

"Is offering to leave Kavya's wish or her helplessness? "Indra paused. The profoundness of the question hit Dave. Indra could sense the growing tension. She let the silence last long enough, the uneasiness to speak for itself.

"But Indra, we can't bend the rules for everyone. If we make exceptions, it sets a bad precedent. Others also have their life issues and will start demanding similar accommodations, and honestly, the work can't suffer." Dave stiffened in his chair.

Indra took a deep breath, steadying herself. "Dave, I hear your concerns. Let's take a step back. Kavya isn't asking for a free pass—she's been managing her responsibilities and excelling despite her challenges. Would you agree?" Dave nodded silently, "Yes," he said, evading Indra's gaze.

"I have seen people getting supported here all the time, Dave. That's who we are. I was supported by Renuka a few years back when Ma had a health scare. Do you remember when you were promoted to lead your first big project? Didn't we support you when you and Joyce were struggling to manage her difficult pregnancy, and you needed flexibility?"

Dave looked taken aback. His gaze dropped to the table. He said nothing, but Indra could sense she had touched a chord. Indra softened her tone, leaning back slightly to ease the tension. "Dave, leading isn't just about standing firm—about making tough decisions. It is also about addressing issues with compassion. Kavya's situation isn't just about her—it's about the kind of culture we're building here. Do we want to be known as a company that turns its back on its people when they need us the most?"

Dave didn't respond immediately. His fingers tapped lightly on the chair's armrest, a sure sign he was deep in thought. "Why don't we pause and think about this?" Indra suggested gently. "Take the evening to reflect, and we can revisit this tomorrow." Dave nodded slowly. "Alright, Indra. Let me think about it." Indra smiled softly. "Thank you, Dave. I appreciate it."

THE INQUIRY CONTINUES

Tuesday Afternoon, 11:00 A.M. – Informal Employee Chats

Determined to further explore her colleagues' inclusion experiences, Indra spent her lunch break speaking with women across teams. The stories they shared painted a troubling picture. One of them, Sharayu from the technical team, recounted how she was passed over for a training program because Ajay and Suresh assumed she wouldn't manage with a young child at home.

"They didn't even ask me," Sharayu said, her voice tinged with frustration. "But why didn't you confront them? "Indra asked gently. Sharayu sighed. "It is all great to talk about inclusion occasionally, Indra. But ground realities differ. Any woman who asserts herself or asks questions is still considered aggressive in this system. "Indra could not wholly refute the point. She had her share of past experiences and was called "Angry Bird" and "The Feminist Crusade."

Another colleague, Shaheen, jumped in. "Why go that far, Indra? Naveen, from your team, is such a jerk… sorry to say that. Have you noticed how he frequently interrupts others, especially his female counterparts, during meetings to "explain" points they have already made?" "It's not just condescending," Shaheen continued, "it makes those women second-guess themselves. And it does not help that the rest behave as if nothing happened."

Indra wondered if the DEI team was capturing this and what they were doing about it. She had to speak to Saumitra, who managed the portfolio as a part of his other HR-related functions. "But charity begins at home, Indra. You must start addressing these issues with your team closer to home." Her inner voice brought in a sense of responsibility.

Tuesday noon: Confrontation with Naveen

The Tuesday meeting was scheduled in Hercules, a spacious meeting room overlooking the race course. The Fintech project title slide is currently displayed on a large digital screen. Indra walked in, coffee mug in one hand, her notebook in the other, her sharp gaze immediately sweeping over the team. Rajiv sat at the far end of the table, as usual, scrolling through his phone absentmindedly. His slightly dishevelled appearance betrayed the stress of juggling multiple projects, though his demeanour remained indifferent.

Vivek swirled in his chair, spinning a pen between his fingers like he had all the time in the world. Sneha was hunched, her bored expression clearly stating she would rather be elsewhere. Naveen sat upright near the screen, his crisp jacket and purposeful posture radiating confidence. Next to him was Aditi, whose nervous fingers hovered over her keyboard as she prepared to speak.

Indra took her seat at the head of the table, placing her coffee down deliberately. She cleared her throat, bringing the scattered attention back to her. "Good morning, everyone. Let's dive in.

We've got a lot of ground to cover." With that, Indra invited Aditi to start the conversation. Aditi leaned forward, her voice steady but hesitant. "I've been reviewing the code integration logs and noticed some irregularities. Specifically, the API calls for payment processing generate duplicate requests—". Before she could finish, Naveen cut in, his voice commanding. "Yes, I've seen that, too. Aditi is trying to say that the API duplicates requests, which could lead to transactional errors. We need to address it by reconfiguring the parameters immediately."

Aditi froze, her fingers still on the keyboard as if someone had hit pause on her. The room went silent. Even Sneha stopped doodling, her gaze darting to Indra, who sat perfectly still. Indra's sharp eyes flicked from Aditi to Naveen, the faintest stiffening of her shoulders betraying her thoughts. Immediately, in a calm but deliberate tone, she interjected. "Naveen, that's exactly what Aditi just said, right?" Naveen blinked, clearly caught off guard. "I… well, yes," he stammered. "But I was just trying to clarify—" Indra didn't raise her voice, but there was no mistaking the firmness in her words. "Aditi explained it clearly. She did not leave any room for misinterpretations that will beg for clarification." She gave a long glance to Naveen.

Rajiv suddenly looked up from his phone. Sneha straightened slightly in her chair, watching the exchange with interest. Indra looked at Aditi, her tone softening, "Sorry for the interruption, Aditi. Please continue." Aditi sat a tad taller in her chair. She leaned forward and steadied her voice, "As I was saying, the issue seems to be…" she shared her thoughts. The room listened intently this time. Naveen remained quiet, his usual air of authority tempered by Indra's intervention.

CONFRONTATION

As the team rose to leave, Indra caught Naveen's eye. "Naveen, can you stay back for a moment?" The unease in the room was almost tangible. Naveen hesitated before settling back into his chair, his confident posture slightly deflated. Indra waited until the room was empty before she spoke. Her tone was measured. "Naveen, I wanted to address something I've noticed in our team meetings."

Naveen shifted in his seat, his fingers tapping lightly against the table. "Of course. What is it?" Indra leaned forward, her voice gentle but firm. "You often interrupt the women on the team and elaborate on their points, even when it's clear they know what they're talking about. Take today's instance with Aditi." And she paused.

Naveen's face flushed, his confident facade cracking. "I… I didn't realize. I thought I was just being helpful," he said, his voice quieter than usual. "I understand," Indra said, her tone shifting to reassurance. "But we all must be mindful of how our actions impact others. We must create an environment where everyone feels heard and respected." Naveen nodded, his discomfort converting to a reflective mood. "Of course, Indra. I am with you on that. I didn't process it that way. But I want you to know there is no ill will. I will be mindful., "Naveen said softly.

Indra smiled gently. "I am sure you will Naveen. Sometimes, we are not very conscious about our impact on our surroundings. We're a team, Naveen. Our strength lies in how we support one another. I know you want the best for the project, and I appreciate your willingness to work on this."

Tuesday Lunchtime: Aditi's Gratitude

Around lunchtime, Indra bumped into Aditi. "Indra, thank you for what you did in the meeting today. It meant a lot." Indra smiled warmly. "Aditi, you don't need to thank me. You did the hard work—you deserved to be heard." Aditi nodded, her voice growing more confident. As Aditi left, Indra leaned back in her chair, a sense of quiet satisfaction settling over her. She made a mental note to herself: Sometimes, Courage and Compassion can be a stronger currency than work itself.

Tuesday Afternoon, 3:00 P.M. – Indra's Office

Indra was reviewing some reports when there was a knock at her door. She looked up to see Kavya standing there, her eyes brimming with emotion. "Hi, Kavya. Come in," Indra said, motioning her inside. Kavya stepped in hesitantly, clutching a folder. "Indra, I just wanted to say thank you—for everything. Both you and Dave have been so supportive. I didn't expect this, but it means the world to me. This job is critical to me, and I promise I won't disappoint you."

Indra could read between the lines. Dave had extended a longer rope to Kavya. Indra stood and walked around her desk, reassuringly touching Kavya's shoulder. "Kavya, first of all, you've earned every bit of this. Your hard work and dedication speak for themselves. Second, it's Dave who championed this for you. He truly values you as a member of the team."

Kavya's eyes filled with tears. "I'm so grateful. I don't know how to repay this kindness." Indra shook her head, her voice firm yet kind. "Kavya, you don't need to feel indebted. This isn't charity—it's the recognition you've earned through your work. Focus on continuing to do what you do best." Kavya wiped her tears, nodding. "Thank you, Indra. I'll never forget this." As Kavya left, Indra felt a surge of pride—not just for Kavya but also for Dave. She made a mental note to let him know how proud she was of his decision.

Tuesday Afternoon, 5:00 P.M. – Dave's Office

Indra stopped by Dave's office later that day. He looked up from his laptop as she entered. "Got a minute?" she asked, smiling. "Of course," Dave said, leaning back in his chair. He seemed relaxed today. "I just spoke to Kavya," Indra said, glancing at Dave. She's deeply grateful for your support." Dave nodded, a small smile playing on his lips. "I've been thinking about what you said yesterday. You were right—it's not just about rules, it's about people." Indra's smile widened. "I'm proud of you, Dave. You handled this with Courage and Compassion, making a real difference." Dave chuckled softly, shaking his head. "Well, I had a good nudge in the right direction." Indra smiled and let the moment do the talking.

BREAKING BARRIERS

The team was gathered to discuss the company's new gender-balanced hiring policy, a topic that had ignited a mix of enthusiasm and apprehension. Indra introduced the initiative. "This policy is not a PR stunt or some effort at tokenism," she said, her voice calm but firm. "It's about bringing diverse perspectives to our teams. I'd like to hear your thoughts."

The room buzzed with murmurs. Vivek looked at Rajiv nonchalantly and continued to flip his pen. Sneha looked around as if she were gauging everyone's reaction. Aditi sat there, lost in her thoughts. But Rajiv sat back in his chair, arms crossed tightly over his chest. His expression was guarded. Finally, he broke the silence, his tone sharp. "Let me be the bad guy here, Indra. Why do we even need this? It's unnecessary and overcomplicates things," he said, his frustration evident.

The room became quiet. Indra held his gaze, unflinching. She took a slow, deliberate breath and spoke, her tone composed. "Rajiv, I understand your concerns. However, these policies do not undermine the existing structure."

Rajiv's frown deepened, but he stayed silent. Indra continued, "Let's discuss the specific challenges you foresee. I value your insight and want us to address these concerns head-on." Rajiv mumbled something about "practicality" and "complexity" but didn't press further. The meeting moved. The tension lingered.

THE PRIVATE CONVERSATION

Later that day, Indra found Rajiv in his office, sitting behind his desk and staring at his laptop screen. She knocked lightly on the doorframe before stepping in. "Rajiv," she began, her tone warm but direct. "Do you have some time to spare? I want to discuss something important?" He looked up, his expression guarded. "Sure," he shrugged. He tried to show indifference but seemed intrigued by Indra's unplanned arrival.

She closed the door behind her and took a seat across from him. "I wanted to talk about the meeting earlier. I sensed there's more to your frustration than just the policy. Am I wrong?" Rajiv hesitated, his defences visibly faltering. "No, it's OK. If the organization wants something, we give them what they want." He sighed. "Something is bothering you." Indra persisted gently. Rajiv got up and started pacing the room. Finally, he paused, came, sat before Indra, and admitted, "I've been here for years, giving my best, and after Anil left, I thought I'd get more recognition, maybe even a promotion. But instead, it feels like I'm being sidelined."

Indra nodded, her expression empathetic. "Do you feel I was picked for this role because I am a woman?" Rajiv became silent and leaned back. He was not ready for such a candid moment. "Hmm, I don't know. I respect you, Indra, and know how hard you have worked. And…" Rajiv hesitated. "And…. I guess ProMax was poor judgment and a career-limiting move for me. I just cannot come to terms with it, I guess. "Rajiv looked down, his face wincing in pain, his shoulders drooping.

"Rajiv. I know how hard you've worked and understand how it feels to be overlooked. It's frustrating, even disheartening." He looked at her, surprised. "But," she continued, leaning forward slightly, "I need you to see something. Your potential hasn't gone unnoticed—not by the board or leadership. You have a track record that speaks for itself. But expressing your frustration, especially in team settings, could be working against you."

Rajiv's face flushed, and he shifted uncomfortably but did not offer to comment. "Rajiv, you are making more foes than friends by being distant, caustic, and unavailable. I don't like seeing you spiral down, especially when I know how well you can manage people and various stakeholders." Indra's voice showed genuine concern. Rajiv sat silently, lost in his thoughts. Finally, he murmured, "You think I'm short-selling myself?"

Indra smiled gently but didn't sugarcoat her words. "All I am saying is that your voice carries weight in this team. You'll stand out even more if you channel your energy into collaboration and solutions. And when the next opportunity comes, I will personally support you. But we must work as a unit, not against each other."

Rajiv sat silently for a moment, the weight of her words sinking in. Finally, he nodded, his voice quieter. "I didn't think of it that way. I've just been… frustrated. I may have also been pretty mean at times. "Ya, many times," Indra faked a disheartened look. But

I will forgive you if you treat me with strawberry cream." Indra looked at him mischievously.

Rajiv loosened. "Is that your punishment if I miss deadlines and commitments as well? In that case, I can bring you one container every day." He smiled. "Oh, then I better get an updated list of demands and bribes." Indra continued to play along with the banter.

After a few moments, she looked at Rajiv and smiled genuinely. "And I appreciate you opening up about this. Let's work on it together. I believe in you, Rajiv. Always have." A small smile broke across his face for the first time that day. "Thanks, Indra. I'll do better. You will see."

THE SHIFT

The next day, during another team discussion, everyone could feel Rajiv's enthusiasm and engagement. He seemed more tuned to what people were saying and acknowledged Sneha's and Aditi's inputs, building on their ideas rather than dismissing them. Indra watched the subtle shift, her sense of pride growing. As the meeting ended, Sneha caught Indra in the hallway. "What did you do with Rajiv?" she asked, her tone curious. "He's… different today." Indra smiled, "Just introduced him to his old self."

Sneha nudged her, "You are on to something, aren't you? Your persona has had a makeover, Indra. You speak differently, and you carry yourself differently. "Sneha said with curiosity. "I try to bring Courage and Compassion daily at work, "Indra brimmed. Sneha was not the only one to compliment her.

The team embraced Friday with a sense of relief and rejuvenation. The launch of Project Zenith was pushing the team beyond its limits. They just had three weeks to go before the launch. Indra hoped this shift in the team attitude would be sustained and serve them well during the crucial weeks. Indra felt a growing sense of purpose as she prepared to write her insights for the week. Courage and Compassion had opened new doors, and she was eager to see where the next "C" would take her.

"Homework is done, OG. Ready for my next dose of wisdom."

SECOND C
MY INSIGHTS

PRACTICING COURAGE AND COMPASSION AS A CHAMPION

- Courage without compassion becomes dictatorial; compassion without courage becomes passive. Together, they create lasting impact.

- Addressing uncomfortable truths requires courage, but guiding others through them demands compassion. Both are non-negotiable for true leadership.

- To champion change, I must courageously confront biases and guide people with compassion toward shared growth.

- Empathy allows me to understand struggles, but courage compels me to act and make a difference.

- Compassion acknowledges individual limitations; courage inspires one to break through and create a impact

- The goal of couragious confronttation is not winning; It is creating inclusive, empowering solutions.

- As a Champion, my legacy lies not in how many conflicts I've resolved, but in how many lives I've uplifted.

The Next Meeting

"Where to, this time, OG?" Indra met OG and enquired with anticipation. Indra looked stunning in her flowy dress and radiant smile. "We will see," OG exclaimed. "Sunanda Mawashi ke yaha chalte hai (Let's go to Sananda Aunt's place)," she told Roopa, her driver.

"So, Indra," she began, her voice gentle yet probing. When was the last occasion that you mindfully practiced Courage and Compassion?" After thinking briefly, Indra said, "Well, it was when I conversed about Uzma with Suresh and Ajay. They were discussing who to send to Germany for a two-month project. Uzma was an obvious choice—she's talented, driven, and keenly interested in such an opportunity. But they dismissed her outright, saying, 'She's a single mom. She probably won't manage. I couldn't let it go," Indra said firmly. "I asked if they'd spoken to Uzma directly about her willingness or availability. They hadn't, of course. So, I insisted they have that conversation before deciding. It wasn't easy, but eventually, they agreed." OG was listening intently, "And…"

"And Uzma was all ready for it. She made an awesome presentation in front of the committee. Her performance blew everyone away."

OG's lips curved into a small, approving smile. "And how did it feel?" Indra felt a comforting warmth envelop her. "It felt… right," she murmured. "As if my voice mattered, as if I could make a difference."

As they moved along the Queen's Necklace, the sun dipped gently into the ocean's embrace, painting the horizon with hues of gold and crimson. "Ahh, here we are," exclaimed OG. "I can't wait to get in. You are going to be blown away, dear. You must also carry a parcel for Akhil."

The food joint for today's meeting wasn't a posh café or a chic restaurant but a rustic vada pav center tucked away in the bustling by-lane near Marine Drive. The air smelled of fried chilies and freshly baked bread, mingling with the chatter of customers who flocked to this place for the divine snack, the soul of Mumbai city.

"What is this place, and how have they restored their Amchi Mumbai (Our Mumbai) vibe?" Indra said aloud. OG was already seated on a wooden bench. She looked serene, almost meditative, as she took in the sights and sounds of the small eatery. "Yes, you said it. This place has a soul, doesn't it?" she said, gesturing toward the women behind the counter.

Indra smiled, nodding. "It's… different. I wouldn't have guessed you'd pick a place like this." OG's eyes twinkled. "Sometimes, it's in places like these that you find the most profound stories." A woman in her late fifties approached their table as if on cue. She was dressed in a simple cotton sari, her hair neatly tied in a bun, and her face radiated warmth and authority. "Ojaswi tai (Sister)," she said with a wide smile, "You're back again! And you've brought company this time." OG stood up to greet her with a familiar ease. "Sunanda, how could I stay away? Your vada pav is as irresistible as your story. This is Indra, my young friend. I want her to hear about your journey and relish your vada pav and missal."

Sunanda chuckled. "Ho Ho (yes, yes). Come, sit. Let me tell you how this little joint started. But before that, let me make arrangements for what you are looking for, Ojaswi Tai." Sunanda smiled mischievously and disappeared to get them the snacks.

Sunanda began sharing her journey as they settled into a quieter corner with vada pav, some hot piping missal pav, and cutting chai (tea). "This wasn't always what you see now," she said, her voice carrying a mix of nostalgia and pride. "Years ago, I started this place with three of my friends. We were all struggling to make ends meet—single mothers, widows, and women abandoned by their families. Kay karnaar? (what could we have done?). We didn't have much, but we had each other."

Indra leaned in, captivated by the earnestness in Sunanda's tone. "We started small," Sunanda continued. "Just one stove, a borrowed recipe, and a dream to support our families. But as we worked together, we realized our struggles weren't unique. So many women like us were desperate for a way to stand on their own feet. That's when we decided this wasn't just about us anymore. And eventually, it converted itself into a movement."

"A movement?" Indra asked, curious. Sunanda nodded. We formed a cooperative and started bringing more women into the fold. It wasn't easy—there were skeptics, naysayers, and even a few failures. But we were consistent, and we were committed. Today, we run 30 outlets across the suburbs of Mumbai, all staffed by women who once thought they had no future."

She took a moment, reached for her phone, and started showing them photographs of her other sakis (friends) as she called them and their outlet.

Indra was intrigued. "That's incredible. This must have been so difficult," she said softly. "Tai, easy things are done by all. But we women are 'Annapurna,' the giver of food and nourishment. And those who are the creators of nourishment for the body, how can you allow their souls to wilt? Who will nourish and nurture them? Who will make them 'Sampurna' (complete and whole)?

The three sat in silence. Indra looked at Sunanda with renewed respect and admiration. Sunanda's face brimmed. "We have been building this community every day, 365 days… for a Taap (12 years) now, "she concluded.

OG, who had been listening intently, spoke up. "Indra, Sunanda is too modest to leave out her achievement. She has been a beacon of hope for almost 350 women thanks to her relentless efforts. She is a regular speaker in forums and at TED-EX talks. I will send you the links to her videos. Amongst the many accolades, she has been bestowed the Aadarsh Mahila (Ideal Woman) award by the Maharashtra government and the Pathfinders award by the Asian Society for Women Empowerment. "Indra was blown over. "Sunanda, your story perfectly embodies what I wanted Indra to understand today—Commitment and Consistency. It's not just about starting strong; it's about showing up every day, even when it's hard, even when it feels like the world is against you. It is living the third C - Consistency and Commitment.

Part 5

TRANSFORMATION

THE THIRD C

Sunanda joined her team behind the counter. OG took a sip of her cutting chai and carefully set the glass down. She leaned forward slightly, her eyes piercing yet calm. "Indra," she began, her tone gentle but purposeful, "If I were to ask you how committed and consistent your organization has been in fostering an inclusive culture, what would you say?" Indra straightened in her seat and paused, thinking carefully. "I'd say… It's a mixed bag. Some moments feel genuine, but others seem more performative." Indra was momentarily distracted by the ruckus created by a few youngsters. "Honestly," she said, her voice low, "it's hard to say they've been consistent. Sure, there are good intentions, but… there's a gap between words and actions."

OG raised an eyebrow, signalling for her to continue. "Can you share an example?"

Indra leaned forward, resting her elbows on the table. "Take me, for instance. A few years ago, I was invited to a high-profile investor meeting. At first, it felt like the beginning of a new era—a woman getting to sit at the table. But when the actual discussions began, they didn't let me speak. I was constantly talked over. The then COO even dared tell me to come "dressed" to make an impression." OG winced, her expression pensive. "I see. And how did that make you feel?" "Angry," Indra admitted, her voice hardening. "Angry because it wasn't fair. And because it sent a message, I was there to be seen, not heard."

OG tilted her head slightly and nodded. Indra continued, "You know, OG, I have a colleague named Arfa. She's brilliant, yet she does not enjoy any true decision-making power. However, management puts her on promotional posters as the face of inclusion." Indra's hands tightened around her, cutting chai glass. "And don't get me started on Women's Day."

"Hmm, it's a Commitment Consistency issue, Indra. "OG said with a pensive look. After a few moments, OG began again, her voice commanding rapt attention. "Commitment and Consistency. These aren't separate traits—they're a continuum. Together, they define how deeply one is dedicated to a cause and how reliable they are in acting upon that dedication. For a cause like inclusion, these elements aren't just essential; they're non-negotiable."

Indra leaned forward, intrigued. OG continued, "Think about it. Anyone can claim to be committed to inclusion, but what does that Commitment even mean without Consistent action? On the other hand, if someone consistently follows inclusion practices but doesn't believe in them, their actions lack authenticity."

OG reached out for a piece of tissue paper; her fingers steady. "Can you think of anyone in your organization who walks the talk? "Indra paused, her face softening slightly. "Yes. There's Ramesh. He's different. He doesn't just talk about inclusion—he lives it. He ensures that women on his team get equal opportunities, whether mentoring, projects, or promotions. He's consistent and genuine."

OG smiled faintly. "Ahh. An Active Ally. Someone who's both Committed and Consistent. Active Allies are leaders who align their words with their actions, creating real change. Their Commitment is unwavering, and their Consistency builds trust. They are instrumental in bringing meaningful change." Indra nodded, a faint smile tugging at her lips. "That's the ideal.

"Hmm, "she said but didn't seem to be listening. She had moved ahead in her head. She continued, "What about leaders who mean well but struggle to follow through?" Indra laughed, "Saumitra, our HR head and DEI champion, is passionate about inclusion but all over the place. He takes on too much at once. He starts initiatives with enthusiasm but doesn't sustain them. The intent is there, but the execution… falls apart."

OG nodded thoughtfully. "A Hopeless Idealist. These individuals mean well. They're deeply committed to the cause, but they fail at execution. They have too many windows on their screens and no bandwidth to do justice to any of them. Their hearts are in the right place, but their heads and hands lag. "Indra's gaze dropped to the table, her voice soft. "That… that sounds a little like me sometimes. I want to do so much, but I get overwhelmed. I start initiatives, but they don't always reach the impact I hope for."

OG did not answer or comfort her with the usual, 'You will get their vibe.' Indra could feel her body tense. "And then there are those who comply, like a tick in the box. I call them "Reluctant Conformists. They're consistent in their actions, but not out of belief. They comply because they have to—because it's company policy or societal expectation. Their actions are robotic, lacking authenticity."

Indra's lips tightened, recalling a memory. "Like when we rolled out that mentorship program for women, but most mentors didn't care about inclusion. They just went through the motions, meeting their mentees because they had to, not because they wanted to." OG leaned forward, her elbows resting on the table.

Lastly, Indra, some leaders don't engage at all. The Passive Onlookers don't even pretend to care. They watch from the sidelines, disengaged and uninvolved. They're silent and detached, as though inclusion is someone else's responsibility. Indra sighed. "I've seen plenty of those too. People oblivious to inequities of life, enjoying themselves in the la-la land."

OG reached out for her bag and brought out another laminated card. "So, let's map this out." She placed the card before Indra.

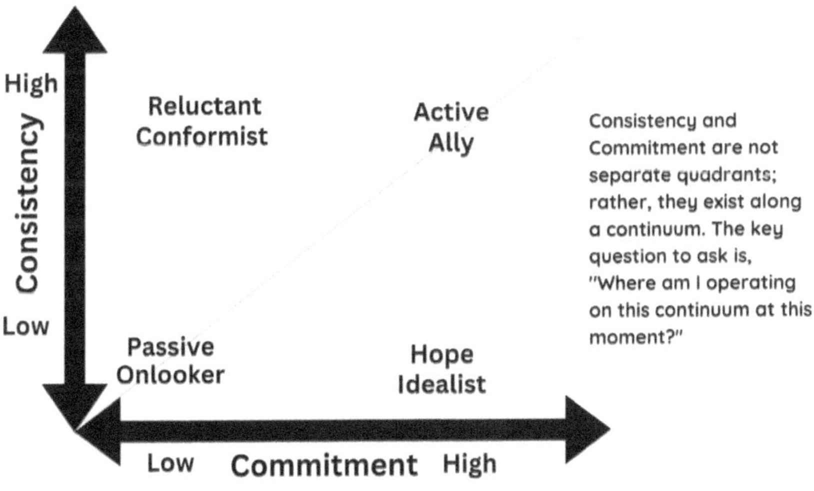

"And now, Indra, I have to ask—where do you see yourself? "Indra started at the card, a million thoughts racing through her mind. She didn't have an answer for this, nor did OG seek an answer from her.

"The truth, Indra, is that this isn't a question we answer once and forget. We all have to ask ourselves this—over and over again. Where we stand today might not be where we stand tomorrow. But if you're not asking the question and not reflecting deeply..." She paused, her gaze unwavering. "...then you're standing still."

OG reached out to Indra from across the table, building an air of urgency. "Indra," she said, her voice dropping even lower, the weight of each word palpable. Inclusion isn't about grand gestures. It isn't about perfection. It's about showing up—every day, especially when it feels the hardest."

Indra sat back in her chair, the noise of the vada pav joint a distant hum now, the scent of fried dough and spices swirling unnoticed around her. She felt exposed, vulnerable—but also strangely alive. The card with its continuum blurred before her eyes, but OG's words remained razor-sharp in her mind. This wasn't just a question. It was a challenge—a call to rise, act, and choose.

Indra felt the unmistakable pull of something far more profound than guilt or regret. It was a purpose—a purpose she could no longer ignore.

FIND YOUR WAY

"OK, let's leave," OG said suddenly, pushing back her chair with a decisiveness that startled Indra. "Wait, where?" Indra stumbled out of her thoughts and jolted back to reality. Before she could fully register what was happening, OG had already stood up, exchanged a few words with Sunanda Tai, and started heading out of the Vada pav joint.

Indra scrambled to catch up, nearly knocking over a chair hastily. "OG, wait! Are we going somewhere else?" OG turned, her face lighting up with a mischievous smile. "I don't know about you; maybe you're off on a hot date?" She raised an eyebrow playfully. "I'm heading back to my dog, book, and cozy little dwelling, Indra."

Indra looked at her, dumbfounded. "No, but what about the third C?" OG paused mid-step, tilting her head as if trying to remember something. "What about it?"

"What next?" Indra's voice carried an edge of urgency. "Don't you want me to practice it next week? How do I..."OG stopped and turned to face her, folding her arms. "Of course, you need to practice it. That's the deal, remember? No practice, no fourth

C." She delivered the words with fake sternness, then broke into a grin.

"But how?" Indra protested, her voice tinged with frustration. "We've completely skipped over the how part today!" OG's face was unfazed. She shrugged. "What do you want, Indra? An instruction manual?" Indra blinked. Indra thought to herself, her frustration bubbling beneath the surface. She sighed, her tone softening. "Is there... I don't know, a best practices book or something? Something that explains how to be Consistent and Committed?" Even as the words left her mouth, Indra felt their hollowness. They hung in the air, empty and weightless. Slowly, the realization crept in.

"You have to find your path," OG nudged, reading her mind.

OG didn't say anything more. Instead, she stepped closer, her gaze steady and filled with unspoken messages. After a moment, she reached out and gave Indra a quick, firm hug.

"OG," Indra started, her voice faltering slightly, "I..." OG pulled back with a knowing smile and held up her hand to stop her. "No shortcuts, Indra. You'll figure it out. I know you will."

As OG turned to leave, she paused and held up the bag she had picked on her way out. The aroma of those yummy Vadas of Sunanda could not be missed. She handed it to Indra with a twinkle in her eye. "Don't forget to take this back to Akhil and Ma," she said lightly. Indra looked down at the parcel, her heart full. She didn't need to open it to understand what it symbolized.

As OG walked away, Indra whispered, "Find your path," gripping the parcel tightly. She didn't have all the answers yet, but for the first time in a long time, she felt ready to start searching.

THIRD C- IN ACTION

The week began with the same humdrum. Indra was stoked that each week looked like the one that had passed. The same aroma of coffee filled Orian, the same agenda points, the same deadlines, the same set of people …. But something was going to be different. Indra was about to take her first step in Commitment and Consistency.

Building Psychological Safety

"All right, team," she began, her tone decisive yet approachable. "Before we dive into this week's agenda, I want to share something on my mind. We talk about innovation—how to build products that stand out and truly serve our users. But we can't create groundbreaking products unless everyone here feels empowered to bring their best ideas forward. So, moving forward, we're going to focus just as much on how we work together as on what we create."

Vivek raised an eyebrow but stayed silent. Aditi, the head of product innovation, exchanged glances with Sneha, the UX lead. It was clear they weren't sure where this was going. Indra broke the silence. "Let's start with brainstorming for the new accessibility feature. Samaira, you've been quiet. What do you think?"

Samaira was a new kid on the block who had joined Aditi's team. She also had a good experience in the UI/UX space. Samaira was taken aback. She hesitated, her fingers nervously tapping the edge of her laptop. "Well… I was thinking… What if we simplified the interface even further? Maybe we should use icons instead of text for visually impaired users?"

Before anyone could respond, Vivek said, "Icons might not work for all use cases. We'd need to validate that first." Indra cut in gently but firmly. "Vivek, let's hear Samira first. Friends, let us follow the ACT formula in the future. People seem lost, "What's this new lingo?"

"ACT stands for:

Attend: listen without interruption, "she said, glancing at Vivek and Naveen sitting beside him. "... and listen for what is being said and perhaps what is not being said."

"Clarify: rather than brush away the idea, probe and clarify, try to understand the other's perspective, and

Think through, look at the idea's pros, cons, and relevance."

The responses were mixed. Encouraged, Samaira explained her vision in detail. By the end of the meeting, the team agreed to prototype her idea for testing. Indra made a mental note to follow up with Samaira later to reinforce that her input mattered. Indra found Rajiv looking at her and smiling. The smile was not a mocking grin but a flicker of admiration and respect. Or so she loved to believe.

Amplifying Voices

Aditi presented her roadmap for the next quarter during a Wednesday demo presentation for a new client. Midway through her presentation, one of the clients directed a technical question to Rajiv, bypassing Aditi entirely.

Indra was watching, and just as she was jumping in to pass the ball back to Aditi, she heard Rajiv say, "That's a great question." Her heart sank. Aditi, would you like to address it? This is your area of expertise." Indra was thrilled with what Rajiv had done. An Active Ally had crept from the bushes.

Aditi smiled gratefully, and Indra looked at Rajiv with admiration. Rajiv looked at her and winked. The meeting went well. After the meeting, Indra approached Rajiv. "Thank you for that, Rajiv. I've had situations like this before, and it almost seemed Aditi would lose her voice, but for your intervention."

Rajiv seemed a bit uneasy, "That was nothing. You are doing something good here. I can see it. I am not such a jerk that I will sabotage what you are trying to build, Mohan. "Indra could sense a lump grow in her throat. After ages, Rajiv called her Mohan; their way of addressing each other by surnames during the good old days of friendship and collaborative spirit.

"In fact," Rajiv, who had walked a few steps, retreated. "I have thought of a nice practice to back up your ACT." "Ohh really," Indra was intrigued. "And what's that?"

Rajiv seemed uncertain, "Let's drop it if you feel it's too melodramatic or something." "Come on, Rajiv, save the preamble. Indra teased. By then, Aditi had also joined them.

Rajiv said, "We should have regular R meetings. "Raise Review Rectify." "Ahh, "Indra exclaimed. Often, we feel it's our birthright to criticize. Those who point out a mistake or raise the concern must partner with us to review and rectify the issue process," Rajiv smiled sheepishly.

"Wow, that's a great idea, Rajiv," Indra said excitedly. "It also helps us to invite all voices and build an inclusive and collaborative culture. What do you think, Aditi?" Aditi seemed floored by Rajiv's brilliance. "That's a fantastic idea, Rajiv; we can add one more R- Recognize those who added value. "Aditi beamed. Indra and Rajiv were impressed." And Rajiv, thanks for passing the ball to me at the meeting. I appreciate it. "Rajiv seemed all red. "Ohh, stop you ladies. Please don't be so generous with your praise. That's what we men don't do often enough," he said, embarrassed. "Then you better start that practice, Rajiv," Aditi called out mischievously as she entered the lift to leave.

Creating Feedback Loops

Later that week, Indra gathered her team for a candid discussion. She started with a confession. "I've realized that as a leader, I don't always know what's holding you back from doing your best work. So, I'm introducing a new monthly feedback loop. You'll get an anonymous survey to share what's working, what's not, and what barriers you face." Some eyes in the room rolled.

Indra added quickly, acknowledging the looks, "I know… I know. Some of us feel that such surveys are a waste. We even complete them as a tick in the box. I have also seen our manager engagement index (MEI) and intend to have a one-to-one discussion with you all, sharing the highs and the lows."

Naveen, the head of data analytics, was the first to respond. "That sounds good, but how will we know the feedback leads to changes?" "Fair question," Indra said. "I'll commit to sharing the survey results with all of you and an action plan based on your input. If I'm falling short, hold me accountable. I will schedule a monthly 30-minute accountability talk with you to share what I did regarding the 3 Cs."

"OK, OK. Now, what's that?" Sneha asked, pretending to be bored and tired of Indra's jargon but, in fact, very curious to know what hacks she was using. Everyone had noticed the change in her in the past four weeks, and Sneha was very intrigued by it. "Hmm, that's a long story. But I can have a quick 30-minute call to walk you through each C per week. Frankly, I don't know what the fourth C is for now. If anybody is interested, join the WhatsApp link I will share, and we can have our 4C Champs group. "That gave birth to a Listening Circle-like platform that Indra would continue to nurture and build over the next few years.

Chat with Vivek

Vivek Joshi, Indra was going through her notes on Vivek. She liked the expertise and composure with which Vivek operated, but that also brought in a degree of coldness and distancing that he seemed to be displaying with his team. He leaned toward being more of a bystander and a reluctant conformist. But Indra felt it was because he was weak in the first C - the Conscious and Curious part. She knew she would have to spend some time coaching and mentoring him.

And that was the birth of the MOM forum (Moments with Mentor) group.

Indra could sense a shift in the team dynamics. It was too early to make any tall claims. Projects were running smoothly for now, and people were less cryptic with each other. She was beginning to feel that the page had been turned over. What lay ahead was a mystery, but what was happening was worth all the efforts.

ONE MORE WEEK

Indra stared at her laptop screen, her fingers hovering over the keyboard. Her inbox was overflowing, and her phone buzzed with constant updates from the Project Zenith team. Launch week was here, and the pressure was suffocating. The stakes could not have been higher. This wasn't just any project—it was a cornerstone of the company's future strategy, and Indra was at the helm.

The board's scrutiny felt like a sword hanging above one's head, and Suresh wasn't making it more manageable. He nitpicked every move she made, his tone sharp, his comments caustic. Meanwhile, Ajay, who had improved, still wavered between being an Active Ally and Bystander.

Amidst this chaos, her phone buzzed while Indra went through the MIS. A message from OG lit up the screen. "Hey, can we postpone our session by a week?" Indra blinked at the message, and her initial reaction was relief. Relief because the thought of juggling yet another thing this week seemed impossible. But curiosity soon followed—it was unlike OG to cancel or reschedule. "Sure, OG. Everything OK?" she typed back, her concern evident in her message.

OG's response came swiftly, "Yes, dear. All good. We have a mega event next Saturday—THEF's annual night—and I barely have time to breathe."

Indra exhaled, relieved that nothing serious had happened, and responded. "Oh, that's OK, OG." There was a pause before OG replied. "Let's meet next Saturday instead. I'm extending an invite for the event—we can catch up during the evening."

"Sure, I'll be there. When do we have our one-on-one for the final C?" Indra was eager to know. OG's reply was immediate but vague, "Saturday, 7:30 P.M. at the venue."

Indra frowned slightly, her fingers tapping the edge of her desk. "I mean our session, OG," she muttered, typing a follow-up. "When do we meet for our one-on-one?" Indra repeated. But the response never came.

The rest of the day swept Indra away in a whirlwind of meetings, approvals, and troubleshooting. She barely had time to breathe, let alone check her phone. By the time she collapsed that night, OG's unanswered message had slipped her mind entirely.

As the days passed, Indra found herself increasingly consumed by Project Zenith. The Third C—Commitment and Consistency—hovered in her mind like an unfinished sonnet. She'd tried to embody it and to reflect on what it truly meant, but the chaos of work made it feel like a distant priority.

But for now, life went on.

STANDING TALL

On Friday, the air in the office was electrifying. Project Zenith's launch had been nothing short of spectacular. Weeks of relentless effort and nights pouring over minute details finally paid off. The launch was finally happening. The company's most ambitious project - a product that could redefine its market positioning—was out worldwide. Indra and her team had played a pivotal role in its success.

A few weeks back, she would have laughed if someone had predicted that she would be standing tall with her team backing her up. But today, it was a reality. All was not perfect, but the journey of excellence had begun. The entire organization buzzed with excitement. Teams cheered as congratulatory messages flooded the group chat. Rajiv was practically glowing. Sneha high-fived Naveen from analytics as they recounted a late-night breakthrough that had ironed out a critical feature. Even Dave allowed himself a rare smile.

Then came the moment that stunned Indra. Suresh, her harshest critic throughout the process, walked over.

"Well done, Indra, you've raised the bar," he said, his voice steady but tinged with respect. The clouds seemed to lift. Indra's heart swelled with pride. Maybe this is the beginning of something new, she thought. "And miles to go before I sleep." She quoted Robert Frost in her head.

REFLECTIONS

That evening, as she sat on her balcony, gazing at the stars, Indra pulled out her notebook. The glow of Project Zenith's success hadn't dimmed, but one more task was her commitment to OG's challenge.

She had already decided to attend THEF's annual event the next day. The 4th C's curiosity was killing her. OG hadn't returned with a slot for their one-on-one session. Knowing how much OG would be immersed in the event work, Indra had decided not to push. "I'll ask her tomorrow, "she thought.

For now, her task was to capture her insights about the 3rd C— Commitment and Consistency.

Commitment and Consistency aren't abstract ideals—they are deeply rooted in actions with others." She thought. It's in the quiet follow-ups. It's showing up fully—not just physically but emotionally—listening, encouraging, and being present, even when the weight of the project felt unbearable. She realized the 3rd C wasn't about grand gestures or one-off acts. It was in the quiet, repetitive actions that built trust and momentum. The 3rd C wasn't something you mastered—it was something you practiced every day. Indra leaned back in her chair, a small smile on her lips.

THIRD C
MY INSIGHTS

PRACTICING COMMITMENT AND CONSISTENCY

- Commitment is a promise you make to others. However, it starts with a promise to yourself. You can't commit to others if you don't believe in your own abilities to fulfil the commitment.

- Consistency is the currency of trust. It's not the big wins but the steady, small actions that matter.

- It's okay to falter. Commitment isn't about perfection; it's about staying on the course, even when you stumble. Resilience is as much a part of consistency as reliability.

- People notice more than you think.

- Small actions compound over time.

- Clarity is the foundation of consistency. It's easier to stay consistent when you're clear about why you're committed.

- Consistency in allyship turns good intentions into lasting impact.

- Commitment to isn't about grand gestures; it's about daily choices.

- One-time support is kindness; ongoing support is allyship.

- The strongest allies don't just react to injustice; they proactively challenge it.

- True leadership is about modeling the behavior you want to see.

THE MEGA EVENT

The day of THEF's annual event had finally arrived. Indra stood outside the venue with a mix of excitement and unease. The atmosphere was electrifying, with a steady hum of energy that seemed to pulse through the air. The place was buzzing with people putting up posters and arranging their displays. The exhibition showcased stories of organizations and leaders transforming their companies into upholders of inclusion. Indra adjusted her sari pallu. Ma finally convinced her to wear her tussar. Indra felt like an alien. She wished she had turned down this invitation and met OG quietly.

"Ah, there you are!" OG's rich, warm voice cut the crowd's hum the crowd. She was dressed in a mustard-coloured saree with a blue and gold border, her bindi back. "OG! I was beginning to think I'd be wandering around like a lost tourist," Indra laughed, relief washing over her face. OG chuckled and placed a reassuring hand on her shoulder. "Let me introduce you to a few folks." She led Indra to a circle of people. After a round of introductions, OG turned to Indra and said,

"We'll meet at 7:30. In the meantime, don't miss the Nukkad Natak. You'll find it intriguing. Indra frowned. "What's that?" OG's eyes twinkled as she explained. "It's a street theatre, Indra. It'll leave you thinking." Indra nodded; curiosity peaked. "What about you? Won't you be joining?" OG waved her off with a smile. "I'll catch you later."

THE THEATRE

At exactly 5:30, the Nukkad Natak began in a small courtyard outside the auditorium. The performers stood on a makeshift stage, the actors engaging with each other, their expressions animated, their voices echoing with intensity.

Scene one: A pregnant woman in a job interview, her qualifications superior to other candidates. Yet, the interviewer, a man in his mid-40s, hesitated. "What happens when the baby comes? You'll need months of leave. Honestly, hiring someone like you is just too risky." The pregnant woman's shoulders sagged under the weight of those words. And the facilitator said, "Cut."

Scene two: A group of men joked and laughed at the expense of a female colleague, their words toeing the line between casual humour and harassment. She sat there, visibly uncomfortable. The tension built as one of the men touched her shoulder, and she stiffened but said nothing. "And cut."

The tension was palpable, and the audience shifted uncomfortably in their seats. One of the actors stepped forward and addressed the audience directly. "Now, tell us—what should be the climax? How do we resolve these situations? What would you do if you were in the shoes of these characters?"

A wave of murmurs swept through the crowd. People hesitated, unsure if their suggestions would be heard or judged. Slowly, hands began to rise.

A woman in the audience suggested that the pregnant woman confront the interviewer with facts about workplace policies and the benefits of diversity. Another attendee proposed that the female leader call out the double standards during her feedback session. The audience grew more animated, their suggestions becoming bolder, more engrossed.

The actors improvised, incorporating the audience's ideas into an unscripted conclusion. The audience applauded, a collective acknowledgment that change begins with individual actions and courage.

As the applause subsided, a facilitator stepped onto the stage. She had a calm demeanour and a voice that carried warmth and authority. "What you just saw was more than a performance," she began, her words drawing everyone in. "It was a reflection—a mirror held up to our workplaces, our behaviours, and, most importantly, our biases. Conscious Curiosity is empty without Courage and Compassion," she explained. It isn't just about noticing biases; it's about questioning them. It's about asking yourself why you feel a certain way about someone. Inclusive leadership isn't passive—it's an active process of challenging our assumptions and seeking to understand perspectives different from our own."

Indra sat transfixed, the facilitator's words resonating deeply. As the session ended, Indra realized that the Nukkad Natak wasn't just a performance but a catalyst that ignited awareness and introspection.

STORIES OF TRANSFORMATION

By 6:00 P.M., the grand auditorium buzzed with anticipation. Indra took a seat near the middle row. The stage was lit with a soft golden glow, casting a halo around the podium as the first keynote speaker stepped forward.

Indra spotted the Aikido maestro, whom Indra recognized instantly from their encounter at the wellness studio, exuding a calm strength. Dressed in a simple yet elegant kimono-style suit, Maestro Akari commanded the room with her presence even before she began speaking.

Her story unfolded with vivid details of her journey in martial arts and the corporate world. "In Aikido," she continued, "we don't attack. We redirect energy. We don't overpower; we align. Leadership is no different. It's not about crushing when faced with resistance—whether from others or within ourselves. It's about embracing it, understanding it, and transforming it."

The maestro's voice dropped to a quieter, almost meditative tone. "Courage," she said, "isn't just in the bold moves. It's in the quiet decisions. It's in speaking up and making hard choices that might not make you popular but will make you proud." She paused, her gaze sweeping the room. "True Courage is lifting others as you climb."

When the Aikido maestro finished, the applause was thunderous, and the impact of her words lingered.

THE PANEL DISCUSSION

The most stirring session of the evening unfolded as a panel discussion under the dim, warm glow of the stage lights. Indra leaned forward in her seat, fully engrossed as a group of extraordinary women leaders took their places on stage. Each of them had reshaped their organizations through deliberate, thoughtful actions.

The first panellist, a soft-spoken yet resolute HR leader, spoke of introducing mentorship programs explicitly designed for women re-entering the workforce after maternity leave. "It's not just about giving women a seat at the table," she said, her voice firm, "but ensuring they have the confidence and support to speak up once they're there."

Another leader—the CEO of a mid-sized tech company—shared how they had overhauled their recruitment policies to eliminate unconscious biases. "We removed identifiers from resumes, conducted blind interviews, and focused solely on skills," she said. The results were astounding—not just in gender balance but in the quality of ideas flowing into the organization."

The stories poured in, each unique yet united by a common thread: Consistency. These weren't grand, one-off gestures but small, intentional steps taken daily, year after year.

But the air in the room grew even heavier with emotion when the spotlight shifted to the next speaker—a woman who had dedicated her life to working with survivors of acid attacks and daughters of sex workers. Dressed simply in a vibrant saree, her presence was understated yet commanding. Her voice trembled slightly as she began, but the conviction in her words silenced even the faintest whispers in the auditorium. "Commitment and Consistency," she said, "aren't just workplace principles. They're deeply personal. They're about staying when it's easier to walk away. They're about believing in someone's potential even when the world has given up on them."

She spoke of teaching survivors how to dream again and of helping them unlearn the shame society had imposed on them. "Transformation doesn't happen overnight," she continued. It's a slow process of holding someone's hand until they're ready to let go and fly independently."

As her words echoed through the auditorium, Indra felt her chest tighten, tears welling in her eyes. This wasn't just a professional lesson but a profoundly human one. The woman concluded her story with a simple yet profound truth: "When you stay committed to someone's growth, you're planting seeds—not just of their transformation, but of a kinder, more inclusive world."

The room erupted into applause. Indra felt the weight of those stories settles in her heart, not as burdens but as inspirations.

THE FOURTH C UNVEILED

The final session of the evening had a fitting title: Culture Custodians—The Leaders Who Made a Difference.

The auditorium glowed with the room's soft lighting and the attendees' radiance. This was a moment for the awardees to shine. Their families were seated near the stage. Their pride and happiness spoke volumes of this honour's meaning to them.

These were individuals who had not only embraced inclusive leadership but had embedded it into their organization's DNA. Each name was accompanied by a brief story of their impact: a finance director who championed policies for flexible work hours, a factory manager who redefined safety standards to include women employees' unique needs and a team lead who ensured LGBTQ+ voices were represented in every project.

Indra was awed by the stories of the people receiving the awards that evening. These were ordinary people showing extraordinary commitment toward Inclusion and belongingness. And then it hit her like a bolt of lightning—the 4th C—Custodianship.

It had been staring her in the face all along. These leaders weren't merely implementing strategies; they were safeguarding values.

They ensured that inclusivity wasn't just a buzzword but a living, breathing reality. Indra's thoughts swirled with admiration and determination as the applause thundered for the final honouree.

A sudden tap on her shoulder broke her train of thought. Turning, she found OG grinning at her, her eyes sparkling with the mischief of someone who knew precisely what Indra had just realized.

"We have a date, remember?" OG said, motioning toward a quieter corner of the venue. Indra smiled back, nodding. Her heart felt full, her mind alive with the day's lessons. She felt the 4th C would bring everything together in ways she had never imagined. But for now, she was ready to listen, learn, and embrace whatever wisdom OG was about to share.

CUSTODIANSHIP

OG and Indra found a quiet nook in the lounge, the distant hum of conversations serving as background music to their moment. Indra turned to OG, her eyes searching. "The 4th C... it's Custodianship, isn't it?" OG smiled softly, the kind of smile that spoke of quiet pride. "It is."

She paused and then asked intently, "Tell me, Indra, what does Custodianship mean to you?" Indra hesitated. "It's... responsibility, right? Doing the right thing, even when no one is watching. Setting the tone for others to follow." OG leaned forward, her voice steady yet warm. "It's more than that. Custodianship isn't just about doing—it's going beyond; it is to RAISE the bar.

Indra gave her a thoughtful look, "RAISE?"

"Yes, Indra, RAISE. Today, I will park with you for a final gift. It is not a cheat sheet or a code. It is a set of values. "Indra was lost.

OG continued. "The first element is the ROLE MODEL. Custodians lead by example. They walk the talk, even when it's tough." Indra let the words sink in, "Like the CEO we heard earlier," she said slowly. "The one who didn't just talk about equality—she completely overhauled hiring practices. She set the example, even when it meant facing resistance."

Indra tilted her head, her mind racing.

OG's eyes sparkled. "The second element is ADVOCATE. Do not wait for someone else to take the lead. Advocates use their voice for those who feel unheard, whether in the boardroom or at the grassroots level." Indra could join the dots. "Like the leader who fought for flexible work policies for young mothers. She didn't just understand their struggles—she stood up for them."

Suddenly, Indra's face lit up. "And I... INFLUENCE, right? That's what leaders do—they shape the culture." OG smiled, "That's correct. Influence isn't about control; it's about inspiring. Like the dignitary who created leadership pathways for women. She wasn't just sitting at the top—she was building a staircase for others to climb."

Indra's chest tightened. "And then there's S—SPONSOR. That one hit me the hardest. The woman who works with acid attack survivors... she didn't just support them from the sidelines. She gave them opportunities, visibility, and the belief that they could rebuild their lives. That's... that's everything."

Indra blinked rapidly, her voice catching. "And E? EMPOWER?" OG's smiled radiantly. "Wow, you are on fire today. Empower. It's about giving people the tools, the confidence, and the freedom to lead. Like the women tonight who shared how they empowered young girls to dream beyond their circumstances. They didn't just break barriers; they built bridges."

Indra stood by the auditorium's glass enclosure. The chill from the air-conditioned hall contrasted sharply with the humidity outside, creating a thin layer of steam on the glass. Lost in thought, she raised her finger and traced five letters into the foggy pane: RAISE. Each letter stood for something she sincerely believed in:

Indra exhaled deeply, overwhelmed. "These women... they're more than leaders. They're guardians of culture. They help people rise, and they help organizations RAISE the bar."

Role Model. Setting the standard by leading through actions, not just words.

Advocate. Amplifying voices that often went unheard.

Influence. Shaping perspectives and igniting change.

Sponsor. Championing others and opening doors they couldn't reach alone.

Empower. Enabling others to take charge of their journey.

"Ultimately, that is the blueprint of a leader, isn't it, Indra? OG said softly.

A YEAR LATER

The auditorium excitedly buzzed as the evening moved towards its most awaited segment. Through Her Eyes Foundation (THEF) had once again outdone itself, delivering a breathtaking showcase of stories, performances, and inspiration. But this moment was the pinnacle—the Culture Custodian Awards.

"It is our pleasure to invite Indra Mohan, Head of Product Development, TechVista, on stage."

Indra rose slowly, the golden threads of her Kanjeevaram sari shimmering under the stage lights. The silk swished softly around her as she walked. Indra felt her heart skip a beat as the spotlight turned to her. Her steps were steady but deliberate as she made her way to the stage, each step heavy with the weight of this honour. Her hands trembled. Just then, there was a wave of cheers and shouts from the right side of the auditorium — her people, her world.

Her team clapped and whooped loudly. Rhea cheered the loudest, Akhil's face glowing with pride, and Ma, overcome with emotion, dabbed at her eyes with the edge of her pallu. But what made Indra's throat tighten was OG—standing tall, giving her a standing ovation, her smile wide and filled with quiet pride. This moment was memorable yet humbling. Indra accepted the plaque with trembling hands. The polished surface reflected her face back at her, but it wasn't just her reflection she saw—it was the reflection of a year of transformation.

As she stood at the podium, she paused. She was too emotional for a speech, but she steadied herself, gulping the lump in her throat, "Thank you. This is not just my honour—it belongs to everyone who believed in me, walked with me, and inspired me to keep going."

She stepped down, her legs feeling weak but her heart brimming with gratitude. OG was still on her feet, clapping with fierce pride. Their eyes met, and in OG's gaze, Indra saw something unspoken—respect and admiration at what she had achieved, a sense of pride for who she had become, and above all, a deep sense of satisfaction with how she had travelled a distance.

And then, as the ceremony continued, the past year flickered through her mind like a highlight reel of transformation and triumph. So much had happened.

Indra had committed herself to THF's She Leads initiative, becoming a member and a fierce advocate. She made it mandatory for her direct reports to mentor others, creating a ripple of growth throughout TechVista. She spearheaded a company-wide DEI initiative, convincing the leadership team to tie inclusion metrics to business goals. This wasn't just talk—it was action. Recruitment practices were revamped to eliminate bias, mentorship programs for underrepresented groups were launched, and unconscious bias training became mandatory for all managers.

Her professional success was meteoric. TechVista had regained its past glory under her watch. Indra's contributions have driven innovation and built a cohesive, high-performing team. Her clients were delighted, and her team was unstoppable. Her team thrived under her leadership.

Rajiv, once an adversary, was Indra's biggest supporter and admirer. Indra had worked closely with him and was his most prominent advocate. When TechVista acquired a major F&B vertical, she rooted for Rajiv as a division head. Today, he was thriving, and his division had already exceeded its targets for the year.

Then there was Sneha. When she decided to move on for personal reasons, Indra didn't just let her go—she stayed in touch, supporting her through her new role. Sneha, in turn, remained a loyal cheerleader for Indra's journey and was here tonight, clapping the loudest. Once hesitant and unsure, Anjali flourished under Indra's guidance and earned a well-deserved promotion.

And on the personal front, her relationship with Akhil had deepened. Where there were once arguments over priorities and roles, there was mutual respect and a true partnership. Even Ma, who had once struggled to understand Indra's ambitions, had softened. "You've always been my pride, beta," she had said just a week ago, her voice filled with love.

Her phone buzzed softly in her lap. She glanced at the screen. Suresh. The same Suresh who had once doubted her now sent a curt but telling message: Well-deserved. Congratulations.

Another message lit up. This one was from Ajay: Congratulations. You are a natural leader, Indra. I wish you great success. Someday, I hope to see you as CEO—sooner rather than later.

Indra has been nominated for an executive MBA at Wharton—a leap she had never dared to dream of until recently. But as Indra sat there, her hands gripping the award, she realized she was still the same old Indra—building her dream brick by brick, climbing one step at a time. Her tower of aspirations was steady, resting on the four unshakable pillars she had embraced over the year:

Conscious Curiosity

Courage & Compassion

Commitment, Consistency and

Custodianship.

She glanced at the plaque again, her vision blurring slightly. Her journey was about more than personal success; it had just begun. The mission was continuing to RAISE the bar.

And then, as the applause for the next honouree roared around her, Indra was reminded of her father's favourite quote from Swami Vivekanand:

"Arise, awake, and stop not till the goal is reached."

The 4 C Model

An Overview of the Model

THE INCLUSIVE LEADERSHIP BLUEPRINT

Inclusive Leadership has become a buzzword in today's corporate world. Why is that so? Is it a new age trend that will soon die its death? Is it the need of the hour, or has it always been an integral part of the Leadership DNA, now gaining the spotlight it deserves?

The quote, "Diversity is a reality; inclusion is a choice," by Stephen Frost, embodies the true essence of Leadership. Organizations are a kaleidoscope of different forms of overt and covert diversities, —manifested in age, experience, gender, sexual orientation, beliefs, personality, and socio-economic class. All organizations are diverse. However, are they, by default, inclusive? Inclusion is deliberate and starts from the top layer, percolating through practices, policies, experiences, and culture.

The core of Inclusion

Inclusive Leadership is not a new-age concept—the idea of co-existing and co-creating lies at the heart of humanity and civilization itself. History shows how leveraging differences and creating harmony has been fundamental to human progress.

A few decades ago, organizations and workplaces were primarily driven by profit maximization, with the workforce viewed as a means to achieve that end. The physical and economic well-being of the workforce was the primary lookout for employers and corporations. Over the years, organizations have become more responsible and accountable for creating an ecosystem that supports employees to feel psychologically safe and helps them get their whole selves to work.

However, Inclusion isn't merely about policies or infrastructure. The experience of Inclusion is in the hands of the leaders who design and weave the culture of organizations. This raises a critical question: How can organizations equip their leaders to create such an ecosystem? One approach to instilling inclusive Leadership is adopting the 4Cs model and making it a core part of inclusion practices.

The 4C Model: Building an Inclusive Leadership Blueprint

The 4C Model offers a structured yet flexible framework that guides leaders toward inclusive Leadership. This Model is not just a set of tools—it is an evolving philosophy, an inside-out approach to leading diverse high-performance teams.

Each sub-system builds over the earlier. In that sense, the Model is an evolving framework where the earlier Cs set the cognitive and behavioural foundation for the next sub-system. It helps the individual to dive deep into beliefs, biases, behaviours, habits, and rituals that make or break the experience of Inclusion for self and others.

Balancing Spontaneity and Structure

Inclusive Leadership thrives on two key processes: spontaneity and structure.

Spontaneity governs most meaningful human interaction. It exists in ambiguity, uncertainty, unpredictability, and irrationality that impact relationships and business outcomes. Structure, on the other hand, provides a method to the madness. Proven behavioural frameworks—such as emotional intelligence, non-verbal communication patterns, and consistent rituals—offer predictability and replicability in achieving inclusive outcomes. Between spontaneity and structure lies the balance of Inclusive Leadership.

From Knowing to Doing: The Inside-Out Approach

Internalizing and embodying each sub-system requires intentionality, actionable goals, and consistent practice. The first two Cs of the Model focus on self-awareness, introspection, and inquiry. The third and fourth "Cs" help leaders go beyond themselves, expand their circle of influence and create an impact.

A Way of Life

The 4C Model offers leaders the tools and mindset to embrace diversity and build an inclusive culture where people feel they truly belong. After all, a need to be included and belong is not a fleeting trend. It is not a business strategy alone. It is a way of life. It is a timeless urge that has always been integral to humanity's progress.

THE FIRST C:
CONSCIOUS CURIOSITY

The first C- Conscious Curiosity is the meaningful analysis of the "What" and the "Why."

Consciousness is about the "What". It entails being aware and mindful of one's bodily sensations, beliefs, self-talk, and body language. It involves building a mindful focus on what is happening at the moment and yet with a deep desire to understand and explore how one responds to the outer world and how others receive or respond in social situations—being conscious means having a heightened state of awareness about oneself, others, and the environment.

Curiosity focuses on the "Why". It is a lens that examines the desires, fears, insecurities, goals, and objectives underlying specific actions, emotions, or responses. Curiosity is the desire to explore and understand the underlying factors influencing behaviour. It is marked by open-mindedness, an intense eagerness to ask questions, and a willingness to embrace new perspectives.

Combining the concepts of self/others and curiosity/consciousness leads to four relational approaches:

Mindful Approach (Conscious Self)

The Mindful Approach emphasizes being aware of one's internal state, actions, thoughts, and emotions and understanding their impact on oneself and others. It involves recognizing feelings, bodily sensations, non-verbal behaviours, and the thoughts that arise in the present moment. The main attributes of a Mindful people are:

- Highly aware of personal emotions, thoughts, and actions.

- Cognizant about the alignment between their intentions and actions.

- Receptive to the emotional responses of others and able to adapt one's response to suit the context.

Reflective (Curious Self)

The Reflective Approach refers to an individual's active assessment and analysis of the thoughts and emotions that govern their behaviours and interactions. It is about being open and curious about their deep-seated beliefs fears; and the main attributes of a Reflective person are:

- Interested in diving into their internal world to learn about themselves.

- Open to self-related information without being defensive or defeatist.

- Reflective on past actions and decisions to foster growth.

Attuned: (Conscious Others)

An Attuned Approach is noticing other people and tuning in to their emotions, needs, and perspectives. Attuned people can objectively process the behaviours of others without filtering them through preconceived notions or biases. They are highly self-monitoring individuals and can adjust their reaction patterns to others' behaviours. The main attributes of an attuned person are:

- Deeply aware of others' emotions, needs, and concerns.

- Mindfully engages with others in ways that respect their emotional states and perspectives.

- Cultivates positive relationships by being emotionally attuned and responsive.

Empathetic: (Curious Others)

The Empathetic Approach refers to the ability of individuals to acknowledge and appreciate others' perspectives and respond accordingly. It helps them to learn about others' emotions and maintain a balance by keeping a rational focus on the goal or objective at hand. The main attributes of a mindful person are:

- Actively listen to others without interrupting, aiming to understand rather than judge.

- Seek diverse perspectives to build a more comprehensive understanding of people.

- Engages in open-minded conversations and is curious about others' experiences.

- Each of the four approaches—Mindful, Reflective, Attuned, and Empathetic—offers a pathway to fostering deeper connections within oneself and others, leading to a more inclusive, thoughtful, and impactful way of interacting with the world.

SELF-ASSESSMENT

Conscious Curiosity

The following self-assessment is designed to assist readers in rating themselves on the four approaches: Mindful, Reflective, Attuned, and Empathetic. The assessment is a self-reflection tool and does not indicate any particular personality type. Readers can use this tool to analyse their behaviours in specific situations and recalibrate them to achieve better relational outcomes.

Rate yourself on a scale of 1 to 5 for each statement, where 1 = Rarely True, 2 = Occasionally True, 3 = Sometimes True, 4 = Often True, 5 = Always True.

Mindful Approach (Conscious Self)

This section helps you assess your awareness of your internal state and how your behaviours align with your goals.

1. I know my emotions, thoughts, and bodily sensations and can notice how they influence my interactions in a given moment.

2. I reflect on how my behaviours influence my personal and professional goals.

3. I identify my emotions and can regulate my emotional expressions in trying situations.

4. I remain calm and composed while dealing with resistance from others or unforeseen challenges.

5. I can analyse the impact of my verbal and non-verbal behaviours on interpersonal interactions.

Total Score for Mindful Approach: _________

Reflective Approach (Curious Self)

This section evaluates your alignment with your inner world and ability to explore your cognitive, emotional, and behavioural patterns that influence your overt reactions.

1. I actively seek to understand my motivations, strengths, and weaknesses.

2. I am open to feedback about myself, even if it challenges my beliefs.

3. I reflect on my past actions and decisions to learn and grow.

4. I am curious about how my fears or insecurities influence my behaviours.

5. I am willing to embrace new experiences that challenge my comfort zone.

Total Score for Reflective Approach: _________

Attuned Approach (Conscious Others)

This section assesses your ability to notice others' emotions and reactions and meaningfully respond to them non-judgmentally.

1. I can accurately perceive others' emotions, even when they are not explicitly expressed.

2. I process others' behaviour objectively, without preconceived notions or biases.

3. I adjust my communication style to match others' emotional states and perspectives.

4. I am mindful of how my actions impact the people around me.

5. I foster positive relationships by being emotionally responsive and respectful.

Total Score for Attuned Approach: _______

Empathetic Approach (Curious Others)

This section assesses your openness and receptiveness to others' opinions and perspectives.

1. I actively listen to others without interrupting or judging their viewpoints.

2. I am curious to know and understand the emotions, experiences, and perspectives of others.

3. I appreciate and learn from people's diverse views and preferences.

4. I engage in conversations that help me understand others' needs and goals.

5. I balance empathy with a rational focus on achieving shared objectives.

Total Score for Empathetic Approach: _________

Interpreting Your Scores

(Score: 5–10 = Needs Urgent Improvement, 11–15 = Developing, 16–20 = Mastery)

5–10: Needs urgent attention – This approach may not be your strong point and may require conscious efforts and strategies to internalize the approach.

11–15: Developing – Your current competence in managing this approach is reasonable. You may benefit from practicing the behavioural elements more mindfully and consistently.

16–20: Strong – You are acing this approach and should focus on leveraging this strength for a more significant impact.

Points to ponder:

- Which approach scored the highest for you, and how does it help you personally and professionally?

- Which approach scored the lowest, and what steps can you take to strengthen it?

- How can you integrate all four approaches to build a more substantial influence on your stakeholders?

- What practices can you think of to help you consistently build the four approaches?

Take either this or the next, but it should be black and white

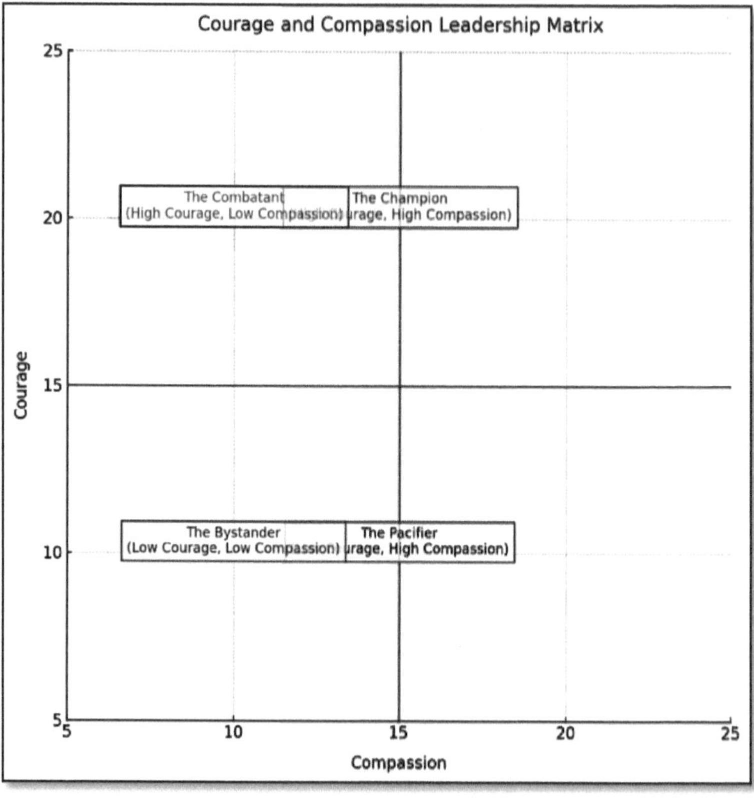

THE SECOND C

COURAGE AND COMPASSION

Courage and Compassion are the two elements that govern what people do in social situations. In the context of Inclusive Leadership, Courage is the ability to take a stand. It involves taking tough decisions and unpopular measures. Compassion is articulating tough or unpopular messages in a non-judgmental and empathetic manner. It is being open to acknowledge others' perspectives while assessing a situation or dealing with an impasse. The interplay between Courage and Compassion gives rise to four types of styles of leaders:

1. The Champion (High Courage, High Compassion)

Champions have an incredible ability to combine candour with kindness. They display extraordinary conviction and confidence to stand for what they deeply believe in. Simultaneously, they are genuinely interested in understanding others' realities and care about people's opinions and feelings. With high Courage and Compassion, they can do justice to themselves, others, and the cause they are engaging with the stakeholders. They inspire others and can become change agents.

2. The Combatant (High Courage, Low Compassion)

Combatants are driven by high Courage and low Compassion and tend to be aggressive and inflexible. They are fearless and risk-taking. However, others may view their style as abrasive and hurtful. They come across as cold and non-adaptable. Their ability to acknowledge others' concerns and emotions is low, making their decisions one-sided and sometimes biased. Their demanding approach and lack of emotional support hinder the creation of deep, trusting relations with others.

3. The Pacifier (Low Courage, High Compassion)

Pacifiers are kind and caring. They can demonstrate great emotional support. However, they may not challenge the status quo or take a stand for others. They are non-confrontational and may not be able to address wrong-doings. They like operating from their comfort zone and lean towards stability rather than confrontation.

4. The Bystander (Low Courage, Low Compassion)

Bystanders may neither take bold action nor show care for the emotional needs of others. They may come across as detached, passive, and self-absorbed. They cannot inspire others or help organizations evolve in the face of change. They do not like to address or fix issues unless there is a dire urgency.

Courage and Compassion influence leaders' behaviour and actions in situations that call for intervention and inquiry.

SELF-ASSESSMENT

Courage And Compassion

Rate yourself on a scale of 1 to 5, where 1 = Rarely, 2 = Occasionally, 3 = Sometimes, 4 = Often and 5 = Always. Add the total Score for Courage and Compassion. Add up the scores of statements 1 to 5 for the Courage score. Add up scores of statements 6 to 10 for Compassion Score. The scores will range from 5 to 25 for each section.

Courage

How often do you:

1. Take bold, unpopular steps, even if they might discomfort you or others.

2. Challenge decisions you believe are unfair, even at personal or professional risk.

3. Propose risky ideas despite the possibility of pushback and displeasure of others.

4. Confront complex issues directly and assertively without avoiding conflict.

5. Take tough stands to achieve personal and professional goals and objectives.

Total Score: _________

Compassion

How often do you:

1. Pause to understand others' perspectives and feelings, even when you have a different viewpoint.

2. Demonstrate care and empathy through your body language and tonality when carrying out crucial conversations or communicating unpopular decisions.

3. Listen actively to others' concerns without judgment or interruption.

4. Adapt your communication style to address others' emotional needs during challenging situations.

5. Acknowledge others' efforts and emotions with genuine appreciation.

Total Score: _________

Plot yourself on the two-by-two matrix to reflect on your interaction style.

Points to ponder

- Do you spend enough time in the Champion zone?

- What one thing you are doing regularly to operate in the Champion zone

- What one thing would you like to practice that will strengthen your Champion Zone?

THE THIRD C – COMMITMENT AND CONSISTENCY

Commitment and Consistency are the bedrock of sustainable measures towards Inclusion.

Commitment towards Inclusion is the degree to which leaders translate intentions into actions. Committed leaders will ensure they follow the organizational norms around Inclusion. They take action to welcome diverse views, comply with DEI initiatives, and demonstrate their support for inclusion efforts. Consistency is the degree to which leaders demonstrate inclusive behaviours over time. Their efforts are consistent rather than being episodic.

Leaders fall into one of the four patterns based on their Commitment and Consistency levels.

Active Ally (High Commitment, High Consistency):

An Active Ally is wholeheartedly committed to inclusivity and takes consistent action to create an inclusive culture within teams. They become the voice of those unheard, advocate for, and handhold the marginalized. Their commitment is unwavering, and their actions stem from their deep sense of conviction and responsibility.

Hopeless Idealist (High Commitment, Low Consistency):

Hopeless Idealists believe in and are committed to the cause of inclusivity. Their intentions are noble, and they endorse principles of fairness and equity. However, they struggle to translate their intentions into consistent actions. Their efforts may look episodic and spurious. They may be unable to sustain their efforts to create long-term impact or change.

Reluctant Conformist (Low Commitment, High Consistency):

Reluctant Conformists consistently follow protocols and inclusion policies defined by the organization. Their efforts are consistent, but their conviction towards the efforts is low. Their involvement and attachment to Inclusion practice is poor. They are driven by organizational agenda and external factors rather than intrinsic belief in inclusivity.

Passive Onlooker (Low Commitment, Low Consistency):

Passive Onlookers do not care about Inclusion. They remain detached and disengaged from the cause and the actions required to drive inclusivity. They are neither intentional nor action-oriented towards DEI initiatives. They believe that feeling included is the responsibility of those seeking such Inclusion or, at best, the responsibility of HR or the DEI team.

Together, Consistency and Commitment in efforts toward inclusivity will make organizations progressive.

SELF-REFLECTION

Commitment and Consistency

Read the following case vignettes and circle the behavioural options that you may demonstrate in the given situations. Please answer honestly.

Meeting

You're in a meeting where a junior team member is sharing ideas. However, others repeatedly interrupt them, and their ideas are undermined and scraped without discussion. You notice the team member becomes quiet and withdraws. What would you do?

Options:

A. Find an opportunity to intervene during the meeting, draw attention to a team member's idea, and redirect the conversation to the junior team member.

B. Talk to the team member after the meeting. Express appreciation of their ideas and reinforce their relevance.

Tell them not to pay attention to disrupters and encourage them to continue contributing.

C. Look for similar patterns in future meetings. If the issue persists, let the head or HR know about such behaviours and request them to look into

D. Continue with the meeting. After all, such interruptions are expected. The junior team members will learn to deal with such behaviour over time.

Hiring

During a hiring discussion, a panel member expresses discomfort with a candidate's suitability and mentions that the candidate may not be a "cultural fit." The member gives no further explanation of the data for this assessment. The candidate meets all the criteria. What would you do?

Options:

A. Ask the panel member for specific data points or information to support their view.

B. I decided to have an informal chat with the panel members to check their perceptions and continue with the other candidates for now.

C. Ask the panel members to fill in a written summary to justify their stand so that the opinion is documented.

D. There are many more candidates. Go to the following candidate profile for discussion.

Taking Credit

In a critical presentation, a senior colleague takes credit for ideas contributed by another female colleague. She is shocked but keeps silent. You notice that she becomes quiet and disengaged. What would you do?

Options:

A. Find a way of getting into the conversation and acknowledge the team member's contribution. Make it a point to speak to the senior colleague after the meeting and check their perspective.

B. Note this and speak to the team member after the meeting. Acknowledge her contribution and promise you will appreciate her efforts in the subsequent mail.

C. Let the meeting get over and then mail formally to all, reiterating appropriate meeting etiquette. Highlight that people should share credit wherever due.

D. Be patient with the senior colleague. This may not have been done on purpose. There would be many more occasions to acknowledge the female colleague.

Stereotypes

During a team meeting, a colleague mentions, "Don't trust these numbers. Do your cross-checking. After all, we all know how women are with numbers." looking at the female colleague who has worked on the report. Others laugh, and a few chuckles. Some look uncomfortable, and the female colleague looks angry. What would you do?

Options:

A. Calmly mention that we should refrain from making such comments, even if they seem friendly banters. Highlight that such comments can look like microaggressions against some team members.

B. Feel disappointed at your colleague's cheap sense of humour. Decide not to highlight the behaviour, fearing it will only put the bad behaviour in the spotlight and disgrace the discussions.

C. Keep quiet. Report the incident to HR and document it formally if it happens again.

D. Stay silent. You are sure that the colleague had no malice while saying this.

Decisions

You have observed that many team meetings continue during informal smoke breaks, and the conversation progresses from where it was formally left. This group usually returns with a final decision and informs these absent about the conclusion. What would you do?

Options:

A. Clear down this behaviour and suggest that the team should refrain from such behaviours. I decided that the meeting would restart at the point where it was left.

B. Check the feelings of those excluded from the conversation. Express your understanding of their feelings and avoid addressing them directly.

C. Let all the team members know that all decisions should follow a formal discussion and document your reiteration of the point via mail.

D. You know that the ones excluded are good friends of the team that takes the smoke break. Assume they will sort things out and not blow this out of proportion.

Scoring and Interpretation

For each scenario, check your responses and assess which is your dominant style:

If you have mostly answered A, your style is that of an Active Ally: You sincerely believe in Inclusion and consistently demonstrate behaviour that reflects your belief.

If you have mostly answered B, your style is that of a Hopeless Idealist: Your heart is in the right place. You consistently feel for the person. However, you struggle with following through and implementing changes consistently.

If you have mostly answered C, your style is that of Reluctant Conformist: You comply with policies and like to document instances. However, you don't like to get personally involved. You are consistent with your behaviour but may not demonstrate the commitment to impact change.

If you have mostly answered D, your style is that of Passive Onlooker: You don't like to engage in the inclusion efforts or feel strongly about them. You are neutral about Inclusion and feel such actions deflate the situation. You would rather stay away from such actions.

THE FOURTH C – CULTURE CUSTODIANSHIP

Culture is an extensively researched and much talked about concept. Culture has been studied through various lenses, such as anthropological, sociological, behavioural, and many more. Triandis, a pioneer of cross-cultural psychology, has defined culture as a phenomenon consisting of "shared attitudes, beliefs, norms, roles, and values that are organized around a central theme and that influence the behaviour of individuals in a society." In the context of inclusivity in the workplace, this would amount to the shared meaning that individuals would create, imbibe, and role model with the organization.

Merriam-Webster defines Custodian as the "one that guards and protects or maintains." In that sense, Culture Custodians under inclusive Leadership are those individuals or groups of people who have the skill and the will to preserve, protect, and promote values, practices, and rituals that strengthen the experience of Inclusion and belongingness within the organization. The fourth C has been crystallized in the form of the acronym RAISE. The Model is a value proposition that simplifies a complex and abstract phenomenon like

Culture custodianship into specific observable and measurable behaviours that can go a long way in building an inclusive ecosystem within the organizations.

The R.A.I.S.E. model emphasizes active, intentional leadership behaviours that promote gender equity in an organization.

Role Model

Inclusive leaders embody inclusive behaviour and set a powerful example of what it takes to be a respectful, unbiased, and fair leader. They demonstrate inclusive behaviour consistently and influence other stakeholders to follow their set example.

Advocacy

Advocacy is the intentional intervention that drives attention toward gender-related issues. Leaders, as advocates, lend their voices to marginalized groups and take note of issues that may create an unfair playing field for women. They take a public stand and commit themselves to the cause of gender inclusion, backing their intention with concrete actions.

Influence

Influence is the ripple effect leaders can create around them to bring about systemic changes. Inclusive leaders, as custodians, use their formal and informal capacity to influence others and seek more outstanding commitment towards gender inclusion.

Sponsorship

Sponsorship goes beyond advocacy and influence. It is an active effort towards providing growth opportunities for women. Inclusive leaders use their network as sponsors to help women advance to higher roles.

Empowerment

Empowerment is the key to building a future-ready talent pipeline. As custodians, inclusive leaders embrace a growth mindset. They trust their women employees with the autonomy and freedom to explore new avenues. They guide, support, mentor, and empower women to help them make their mark.

In Summary:

The R.A.I.S.E. model is thus a value-driven Organization-wide model that aims to transform workplaces and instil an inclusive mindset that will create a lasting and meaningful impact.

SELF-REFLECTION

Custodianship

Points to ponder

Role Model

- Do I consistently demonstrate respect and fairness to diverse people in my daily interactions?

- How am I challenging my own biases and demonstrating my vulnerability?

- What specific behaviours do I role model for others to emulate?

Advocacy

- When was the last time I actively spoke up to create an inclusive environment in a meeting?

- What policies or practices have I championed to promote Inclusion in the workplace?

- How many internal and external forums do I use so that diverse voices are heard and their perspective is shared?

Influence

- How can I influence others to adopt more inclusive practices in the workplace?

- How am I using my power and position to create an inclusive culture in the workplace?

- How do I hold myself and others accountable for creating an inclusive culture?

Sponsorship

- Who in my network am I sponsoring for leadership roles or high-visibility projects?

- How do I ensure that women and other diverse groups have equal opportunities for career advancement?

- Do I go beyond mentoring to leverage my network to create opportunities for others?

Empowerment

- How do I create opportunities for women and diverse groups to speak up and take ownership?

- How do I ensure all team members feel empowered to contribute and challenge their thoughts and perspectives?

- What Leadership initiatives have I promoted to enable my organization's women and other diverse groups?

- Can I keep these behaviours in mind?

Lead by Example: Display behaviours that reflect inclusivity, such as hiring diverse groups in the teams, seeking feedback, and creating a safe space to speak up.

- **Be Respectful:** Treat everyone with respect, regardless of age, experience, background, gender, or sexual stereotypes.

- **Acknowledge Bias:** Set up a practice for people to call out biases safely.

- **Speak Up:** Challenging policies/ practices reinforcing inequality. Call out intentions and action gaps.

- **Share vulnerabilities:** Talk about your weaknesses for forepaws.

- **Mentor Underrepresented Genders:** Support and guide women and gender minorities, especially in male-dominated sectors.

- **Make Inclusion a part of your core values:** Incorporate equity as a fundamental value in the organization's mission, vision, and strategic goals.

- **Encourage Diverse Representation in Decision-Making:** Ensure a good representation of diverse voices in the room and on various forums.

ON BECOMING AN INCLUSIVE LEADER

"No culture can live if it attempts to be exclusive."
– Mahatma Gandhi.

This sentiment emphasizes the importance of cultural inclusivity. The same sentiment is echoed by thought leaders and practitioners advocating Inclusion in workplaces today. An inclusive mindset is the timeless essence of effective Leadership. As Inclusion and Belongingness take centre stage in organizations, the appeal to create a safe and inclusive culture within teams and organizations has only intensified.

Inclusive Leadership is not merely a cluster of personality attributes or behavioural checklists to adhere to. It is a conscious commitment to embrace difference, stay curious about diverse perspectives, and demonstrate the courage to take decisive steps towards creating an inclusive ecosystem. It is about consistently being at it through policies, practices, and rituals. It is about Consistency—embedding inclusivity through policies, practices, and rituals—so that it becomes woven into the fabric of organizational DNA.

To conclude, Inclusive Leadership is not a destination; it is a continuous journey. As we close, I urge you to reflect on whether you are making a difference and creating a ripple of change every day.